# Early praise for "How to be a Chief Risk Off...

*"How To Be A Chief Risk Officer* i
aspiring Chief Risk Officer nee(
grow into the many facets of the
Ann Latham, author of *The*
*Papers,* and *The Disconnect Principle.*

"This book is an absolute must-read for anyone who wants to pursue a career in risk. It also provides valuable insights for any executives and Board directors who ask themselves about the value of risk management."
Julien Haye, Global Head of Non-Financial Risk, Fidelity International

"Tackling an ambitious topic with gusto and rigour, the author has produced a book that will be visited and re-visited by those in the role and those aspiring to be a Chief Risk Officer – it will become a well-thumbed friend as a source of clarity and common sense; its frameworks lend both definition and reference to those seeking understanding, best practice and, in some cases, justification.

The book's forward-looking approach to the role sets the agenda for the modern CRO and the emerging threats and risks that have accelerated the pace of change, but also the central importance of Risk as a discipline.

Not limited to the CRO, the creation of an effective, working "risk culture" is a critical success factor for all companies – as both Guardian and Champion the CRO is truly a "noble role" - characterised by a 'data-first' reflex that will, in large part, define success as working practices and risk management align to make business better, more successful and safer."
Ian Ewart, Board Advisor, Fintech and Financial Services

"A Chief Risk Officer, like a Chief People Officer, is a role that is tasked with helping organisations to see around corners - to anticipate what might happen next, for better or for worse, and to build the organisation muscle and the practical resources (e.g. policies, processes, people) to deal effectively with it if and when it materialises. In this book, the author captures the most demanding and the most rewarding elements of the CRO's job, and colours in everything in between. Not only a book for current and aspiring CRO's, I would suggest it is one for current and aspiring Chief People Officers to have on their shelf too, for guidance on how to establish and advise high performing risk teams, to ensure they are the best they can be."
Anne Kiely, Chief People Officer, EMEA

"For anyone currently in or about to take up the role of CRO, this is a must read. It's packed full of insights and useful tips and it's one you will refer back to again and again."
Cormac O'Neill, CEO and Chief Tempo Officer, Webio

# HOW TO BE A CHIEF RISK OFFICER

## A handbook for the modern CRO

JENNIFER GEARY

Cover design: Tehsin Gul

Editors: Sarah Busby and Andrew Dawson

Copyright © 2022 Jennifer Geary. All rights reserved.

Published by Kindle Direct Publishing

For more information about the author and further materials, visit www.coo-author. com

ISBN: 978-1-9997683-3-1 (e-book)

ISBN: 978-1-9997683-2-4 (print)

For Conor, Jack and Anna

# About the author

Jennifer Geary is a senior executive with over 25 years of experience in finance, technology, risk and legal, across diverse industries from finance to not-for-profit.

After gaining her B.Comm and Masters of Accounting in University College, Dublin, she trained as a chartered accountant and worked with Arthur Andersen in Dublin and New York. She relocated to London in 2002, where she spent 13 years with Barclays in roles ranging from risk to programme management to governance and control. Having long held an interest in corporate social responsibility and sustainability, she served as COO to Save the Children UK before returning to the world of fintech, as COO and CRO of a fintech startup backed by Santander. Most recently, she was Managing Director, EMEA, of financial services software company, nCino.

Jennifer is also an author, speaker and mentor to emerging businesses and serves as a mentor on the Enterprise Ireland Scale programme. She has attained qualification as a chartered accountant, PRINCE 2 practitioner, CISA and CISSP. She lives in London with her husband, two children and two cats.

# Table of Contents

# Introduction

## Why this book is needed

Five years ago, I set out to write a book on the role of the Chief Operating Officer (COO). The rationale at the time was simple – there was a very thin body of knowledge on this critical role and little reference material for the aspiring or new COO. It was simply a gap in the market; a book that needed to be written. The response to the book has indicated that many others felt the same and have found it useful.

The same cannot be said of the role of Chief Risk Officer (CRO), the other role that I have held. Over the past 20 years, since the emergence of operational risk as a standalone discipline, a large volume of, often scholarly, material has been written on the topic. However, in my research of this role, I couldn't find a book that really captured the essence of the role in a concise and compelling way; which was accessible and user-friendly for those new to the topic, those in their first CRO role or those aspiring to it. This book aims to do just that. It takes the same approach as that in my previous book, starting with the core pillars of culture, strategy and execution. It then marries them with the functional disciplines of the role. Finally, it addresses the main tasks in enabling the risk vision: data and information systems, building a risk team and always being able to keep your head up and see the wood from the trees.

From my first role as an auditor in Dublin in 1997, I have spent my career working in or alongside risk. My years as a financial and systems auditor required me to perform control reviews of clients across multiple industries, in both Ireland and the US. Since then, I have spent over 20 years working largely in banks and recently in fintech, with a spell in not-for-profit. I have taken risk frameworks applicable to global organisations and broken them down to make them relevant for smaller organisations. I enjoy codifying risk standards and processes and making them accessible and relevant to people, explaining the "why" along the way.

## Why risk matters

Managing risk matters. It matters to organisations, which need systematic, appropriate controls that don't stifle them. It matters to the public, who need to trust their institutions. However, most of all it matters to people: to their lives and livelihoods. I have seen risk management done really well, and I have also witnessed some of the very serious consequences that can occur when it goes wrong. When risk management fails, there are almost always consequences faced by the innocent. The role of risk management isn't for everyone – as I explain in the first chapter, it requires a certain kind of person who is willing to take a stand and to not always take the easy path. It takes courage, tenacity and confidence to question popular thinking, challenge the status quo and point out vulnerabilities.

The risk profession is not always perfect, of course. There are plenty of ways in which the risk management community can do better at explaining and helping to manage risk, and I talk about that in the later chapters of the book. However, when done properly, risk management is a true public good, and those who opt for this role, and discharge their duties well, can be rewarded in knowing they are truly making a difference. The world needs excellent risk managers and CROs.

This book starts with a discussion of the CRO role, and the character traits that are needed from the individual for this role, along with some potential derailers. It then covers three core pillars which underpin risk; these are culture, strategy and execution. Then, it gets into the detailed technical risk areas, starting with risk identification, then the risks themselves, what they are, and how to manage them, including the emerging risk of our time, sustainability. Finally, it covers governance, and how the CRO can pull the whole framework together to go from good to great.

I have tried to keep the principles as inclusive as possible and reference multiple industries. However, naturally, my areas of expertise are referenced more than most, so there is an emphasis on financial services and, more specifically, UK and European financial services. However, I also invoke case studies from other industries, including the tech and medical sectors, and my hope is that the principles are helpful to all.

## Who this book is for

As I tried to do with the COO role, I want to decode the role of the Chief Risk Officer; to demystify what is an often confusing and jargon-heavy area for those who are aspiring CROs, new to the role or want to understand the area more. I've broken it down into its constituent parts and provided frameworks and reference materials. The result is an execution-ready handbook that will support people on their journey. This book will be useful for:

- people setting out on their risk careers;
- those stepping into their first CRO position, or looking to round out their risk capabilities;

- non-risk staff looking for an understandable explanation of the discipline; and
- CEOs or board members who are getting to grips with their responsibilities, or indeed anyone who is seeking a better understanding of the risk agenda.

I hope you find this book beneficial, and I would love to hear your feedback. You can reach me via LinkedIn, or you can email me at jennifer@coo-author.com.

# Chapter 1

*The role of the Chief Risk Officer*

*"Defining the role of a Chief Risk Officer is no simple matter. This job requires a range of knowledge, experience, and skill that is rarely if ever found in one individual. Most risk managers have a background in market risk, credit risk, or operational controls. Very few are experts in all three—and that's not all. To be effective, a CRO must possess the "people skills" needed to coordinate risk management activities across the entire institution and to navigate the inevitable realities of corporate politics."* [1]

## Why be a CRO or Risk Manager?

You only have to read the quote above from PwC to see that being a CRO is a highly demanding role. It requires technical expertise, political savvy, people skills and no shortage of fortitude to be able to hold your ground. It demands the ability to balance multiple stakeholder agendas, to think strategically and also to be operational and pragmatic as the need arises.

However, risk roles in general offer highly mobile and attractive careers. Once the principles and approaches are understood, they can be applied in a multitude of settings – from individual projects to multinational corporations. While, inevitably, there will be areas of specialism in different sectors, whether financial services, pharmaceuticals, not-for-profit and others, they tend to use similar principles, which is why a critical risk mindset and risk training are so valuable.

Risk is a growing area, and it's still gaining maturity. Organisations are increasingly realising the need to invest in and upskill professionals who can hold organisations to account while being aware of the company's objectives, identify pitfalls and implement appropriate actions, and keep relevant stakeholders informed.

As a risk professional, you also have the opportunity to contribute to a growing body of knowledge and experience. Risk frameworks need to evolve constantly, for example to take account of new disruptive market entrants or new regulation. If you have an analytical mindset, there is great satisfaction in applying your skills and judgement to new problems, identifying solutions and sharing them with your community of peers.

## The career path to CRO

Although the CRO role is still emerging as a specific career path, it is also gradually becoming better defined and recognised in its own right. Previously, it was primarily a role that professionals from certain backgrounds drifted into. Increasingly, there are specific qualifications available for aspiring risk professionals which reflects the maturing of the profession. At the time of writing, the Institute of Risk Management (IRM) offers a range of qualifications, including:

- an International Certificate in Risk Management;
- an International Certificate in Financial Services Risk

Management;
- an International Diploma in Risk Management;
- a Digital Risk Management Certificate; and
- a Supply Chain Risk Management Certificate.

There are also a range of executive risk leadership training courses available for those at C-Suite or senior level, including at LSE, Judd School and others.

However, there remain plenty of senior risk professionals who have come from other backgrounds, including credit risk, audit and information security, so there are many routes into the area. According to a survey by recruiter Russell Reynolds, 56% of CROs come from the credit risk path, a career with a longer history.[2]

> *"Risk management is still evolving as a profession. The role of Chief Risk Officer and the concept of enterprise risk are still relatively new. Of those in risk leadership roles today, few set out to get there from the start—many came from highly technical backgrounds and, when they began their careers, there were no defined career paths or role models to follow."* [3]

In the analysis of where CROs come from, Russell Reynolds noted that risk, general management and international leadership roles were a desirable combination. However, few CROs manage to combine all of these on their way to the role.[4]

Gender diversity in the risk profession remains poor. According to the same study by Russell Reynolds, only 2% of the top 50 banks (so, one bank!) had a female CRO at the time.[5] *Enterprise Risk* magazine looked at why there aren't more women in senior risk positions in their article on women in risk, and at how well suited the female psyche is to the role. As one of their contributors, Dorothy Maseke, said:

*"Strengths that women have include strong communication skills, attention to detail, high emotional intelligence (ability to read facial expressions, moods) as well as trusting our guts (strong intuition) which helps us when at a crossroads. We are able to make decisions without all the facts at times by simply trusting our very strong gut feeling. These unique qualities make women a 'safe pair of hands'."* [6]

At times, women can lack the confidence that they have the skills to do a role. My hope is that this book, along with the wide range of other resources available, can demystify the role and make it more accessible, to women and people of all backgrounds.

## The characteristics of a good CRO

*"The Chief Risk Officer is a C-suite executive who is tasked with the identification, analysis, and mitigation of events that could threaten a company."* [7]

In order to embrace the totality of the role, a CRO should have an analytical, process-driven mindset, combined with people and communication skills, plus flair and ability to use their imagination too. This is a tall ask and requires both left-side and right-side brain thinking. Most of us will inherently have strengths in some of these areas, and require work to develop the others. Generalisations about personality types are dangerous, as there are always exceptions to any rule. However, below are some of the characteristics I've seen which seem to define the essence of the role, regardless of the individual that takes it on.

### Integrity

Integrity is the cornerstone of the CRO role. The hope is that the rest of your organisation also possesses integrity and that you do not need to be their moral compass, but a CRO without integrity is nothing. This is the one attribute that needs to be innate and unshakeable.

## Collaborative, commercially astute and solution-focused

There are plenty of risk managers who possess so much natural risk aversion that they fall into the trap of only pointing out the pitfalls of any decision; only the things that might go wrong with a proposed course of action. Having identified these, they leave the meeting, workshop or committee with the satisfaction of a job well done. This, in my opinion, is not good risk management and will not advance the organisation. A really good risk manager must remember the reason the organisation is there in the first place and, by collaborating with senior leaders and understanding their needs, help them to take calculated, considered risks in the achievement of their goals, rather than avoid risk altogether.

Russell Reynolds says that:

> *"A commercially-astute risk function is able to consider the business holistically. The Chief Risk Officer who develops a collaborative partnership with the business's commercial leaders, working with them from the start of an issue, provides stronger lateral thinking around the use of these data and insights, better preparing the business to deal with emerging risk factors."* [8]

A complete aversion to risk-taking can be just as damaging to an organisation's prospects as taking too much uncalculated risk. All ventures are risky. No business would be able to get off the ground if they focused only on risk. As Daniel Abrahams says, *"Entrepreneurs focus on opportunity and then consider risk."* [9]

In his book, *Fundamentals of Risk Management*, Paul Hopkin argues that people sometimes view risk as the "brakes" of an organisation but that this is an incomplete and negative view of risk management. Yes, the brakes can be applied when the organisation needs to avoid a hazard. However, risk management is just as important as a "clutch" in times of change, and even as an enabling "accelerator", "*helping the organization embrace strategic opportunities and seek rewards*".[10]

The most effective Chief Risk Officers I have worked with are those with a commercial mindset who can calculate risk, assess where the true "red lines" are, and empower the organisation to work freely within those guardrails.

## Tenacity and bravery

Notwithstanding the above, the CRO must be comfortable to stand alone and have a contrary opinion, even if it's not what others want to hear. There have been times when I have been the sole dissenting voice in the room. All eyes were on me, and I had to hold my ground. There is an inevitable risk of unpopularity that comes with that. You have to be prepared for it and comfortable in your own skin. Of course, you must also be comfortable with having your position and views challenged and prepared to offer the evidence when required to support your position.

## Diplomacy and skill in relationship-building

To be able to hold your ground successfully and have longevity, your peers need to trust you. They need to believe that, if you take a position on a decision, it's for a reason and you've not taken that stance lightly. They need to know you're willing to work with them to find a way to achieve the organisational goals in the right way. They need to believe in you and the fact that you want the organisation to be a success. In the good times, you need to sow the seeds of great working relationships so that, when a difficult moment inevitably comes along, you have plenty of capital in the "bank of goodwill" to fall back on.

A further skill that the CRO must possess is that of conflict resolution and the ability to break down barriers. You can expect that there will be adversarial situations from time to time, where feelings are running high and there doesn't seem to be a mutually acceptable way forward. This is where being able to listen, finding common ground and coming up with creative ways forward becomes important.

## People management and political dynamics

As with all leadership roles, your ultimate success will depend on your people skills and your ability to shape the culture of the organisation. It's important for the CRO to be a developer of people, both within the risk team and more widely. As Dawn Holberton says, you have a key role in "encouraging courage" in the broader organisation.[11] You must set the tone that this is an organisation in which you do things the right way (including doing right by the customer), that you don't take short cuts, that you take the difficult decisions and, finally, that you build to last. These values and touchstones have a powerful effect on the culture of the organisation.

## Humour (if possible!)

This is not strictly essential, and plenty of CROs are lacking in it! However, as Caroline Goyder points out in her book, *Gravitas*, true gravitas and presence comes from being able to take the grand vision and the lofty ideals and combine them with being grounded, self-aware and humble i.e. not taking yourself too seriously.[12] An ability to "lighten up" will help you to achieve this balance and build lasting relationships with your colleagues.

# When CRO might not be the right role

The CRO role requires mental strength and resilience. If you are susceptible to fear in the face of high risk, this might not be the job for you. You will be faced with the full spectrum of worst-case scenario outcomes that the organisation and its management could experience. At the extreme, this could include large fines, career-ending censure, injury, death and jail time. While these are remote possibilities, the spectre of things going catastrophically wrong is always there and needs to be considered rationally by the CRO. While being completely clear-eyed about the risks, you need to avoid falling prey to the anxieties that come with this. Moreover, of course, you are there to help the organisation ensure these things don't happen.

*Risk Management* magazine defined a list of "derailers" for the CRO role outlined in Figure 1.1 below: indicators of certain personality traits that might not be compatible with the stresses of the role.[13]

| Derailer | Description |
|---|---|
| Too detail-oriented | Lacks a big picture view; comfortable in the technical details; needs to recognize when something is "good enough" |
| Not a team player | Works in a silo; struggles to delegate or empower; places personal agenda before the team; will not collaborate with the business |
| Closed-minded | Stuck in the past – "this is how we have always done it"; reluctance to embrace new ideas; lacks external perspective |
| Technical arrogance | Does not listen to the business; overconfidence; technical arrogance; disconnected from the business |

| Wedded to the process | "Tick the box" approach; fixation on frameworks; lack of pragmatism; not agile |
|---|---|
| Focused on the downside | Always thinking about what could go wrong; lack of focus on opportunity; being a blocker rather than an enabler; points out problems but not solutions |
| Lacks confidence | Uncomfortable challenging senior leaders; will not make decisions; fear of getting it wrong |
| Lacks commercial appreciation | Failure to understand the business end-to-end; ignores commercial imperatives; cannot articulate value of risk management to the business |
| Inconsistent | Starter not a finisher – no follow-through; blows with the wind, rather than be led by consistent values and standards. |
| Reactive, not proactive | Lack of / poorly articulated vision; not driving progress or improvement; always in firefighting mode |
| Eager to please | Takes on too much without skills or resources; over-promises and under-delivers; team takes the brunt |

Figure 1.1 "Derailers": Personality traits that undermine the CRO role.

It's important to be self-aware and ensure that you will have what it takes when the pressure increases.

## Key relationships for the CRO

Your success as CRO will also depend on your ability to forge strong relationships with your peers and colleagues.

Some of the key dynamics with the other senior disciplines are outlined below, including what risks they may be responsible for and likely tensions that may arise.

- **Board, audit and risk committees.** The most critical relationship for the CRO is the relationship with the chair of the board, and the audit and risk committees. These non-executive roles are responsible for the oversight of the organisation in general, and the risk function in particular. Having an open and regular dialogue with these key stakeholders, outside of the formal meetings, is highly important. I discuss governance more in chapter 13.
- **Chief Executive Officer (CEO).** While needing to operate with a degree of independence, the CRO usually reports on a day-to-day basis to the CEO. That independence is usually achieved by the CRO having a direct line to the board, audit and risk committees, as mentioned above. They also have the right to present and speak at these forums, unfettered by the CEO. The dynamic with the CEO is crucial. How do they react to bad news, to risks being highlighted, and to roadblocks being put in the way? How do they regard the risk function? How do they deal with challenge? More than anyone else on the executive team, the CEO's respect (or lack of it) for the risk function determines how the organisation will view your advice and guidance.
- **Chief Operating Officer (COO).** As my first book showed, the COO role oversees the daily operational and administrative functions, so it can encompass many disciplines, including operations, finance, people, supply chain management etc. The COO can be a great ally when it comes to execution. They are at the coalface of operations and usually see the first signs of stress and strain in the system (e.g. customer complaints, operational issues). However, the COO is usually also trying to "get things done" as opposed to looking for faults in their approach, and so they can benefit from the CRO offering

a contrasting perspective, calling out issues that they might otherwise overlook.

- **Chief Commercial Officer / Chief Revenue Officer (CCO).** Given their mandate to grow the revenue of the organisation, this is one of the roles most likely to find conflict with the CRO as they will be grasping opportunities rather than critiquing them. However, in my experience, it can be one of the most rewarding relationships if a good balance can be found, driving growth in the organisation in a sustainable way, and respecting each other's views and agendas.
- **Chief Financial Officer (CFO).** The CFO is responsible for the good running of the organisation's finances, managing capital and liquidity risk. Their team also manages day-to-day expenses, payroll and accounts payable and receivable. This is an area of interest for the CRO as a strong financial system is a necessity for the good running of the organisation. Finance is also an area that can be prone to fraud risk. If the organisation trades internationally or uses financial instruments, there is market risk to consider. The CFO is also responsible for preparing the annual accounts and ensuring they present a "true and fair view" of the organisation as a going concern. The CRO's assessment of risks and of the strength of the financial system play into that ongoing assessment. I cover financial risks in Chapter 9.
- **Chief Technology Officer (CTO).** The CTO is responsible for the organisation's end-to-end technology platform, including the underlying infrastructure. Apart from the obvious risks around information and cybersecurity, there are also risks relating to systems failure, third parties and many more. CTOs vary in their level of risk awareness – some will naturally consider risk

management in all the decisions they make; others may require regular reminders of the potential consequences of overlooking risk issues. I cover technology risk in Chapter 8.

- **Chief Information Security Officer (CISO).** Speaking of technology risk, a role that is gaining in importance, and indeed finding its own independent space, is that of the CISO. Some CISO roles have now moved out from under the CTO and report directly to the board or risk committee. The CISO can be a key ally of the CRO, bringing technical expertise, owning cyber and data risk issues, and implementing programmes of protection and improvement.

- **Chief Product Officer (CPO).** This is a role that is gaining particular traction in the digital age. The CPO is responsible for all aspects of the product that is put into the customer's hands. Good design is important to them, and they have to make regular judgement calls that balance growth and scaling with the need for stability and infrastructure. As a result, the role can at times come into conflict with the CRO, and it's important to balance building for today and driving high customer growth with putting down sustainable product foundations for the future.

- **Chief Marketing Officer (CMO).** The CMO is responsible for the organisation's branding, marketing, communications, channel strategy, go-to-market plan and more. It's important that they have a robust process for designing and reviewing all marketing collateral to avoid risk, while not hampering the organisation's agility and freedom of expression. In particular, in retail financial services, there's a legal requirement to ensure that "financial promotions" are fair, accurate and not misleading, and this can be a particular area of risk focus. Finally, the CRO can help the CMO and team to understand data protection risks and build the data-enabling consumer strategies required.

- **Chief People Officer (CPO).** The CPO is responsible for all things related to the organisation's people: attraction, recruitment, retention, development, disciplinary, reward and exit. They usually also cover pensions, benefits and employee relations. Risks around people can arise from the onboarding process, litigation, employee relations issues, mismanagement of grievances, payroll and internal fraud. I cover people-related risks in Chapter 7.

- **Chief Legal Officer / General Counsel (CLO).** Like the CRO, this is another quasi-independent function, that usually has direct access to the board. The general counsel's brief ranges from day-to-day commercial support, contract review and corporate development activity to that of ongoing valued advisor for major decisions. They are usually reasonably aligned with and complementary to the risk area, as long as the levels of risk aversion are similar. Legal risk is covered within the operational risks in Chapter 10.

- **Chief Sustainability Officer (CSO).** An emerging role, the CRO and CSO often find a lot in common. Both are looking at the future, at potential risks and at ways the organisation will need to evolve to meet them. Both should also be looking at how they can lean into sustainability, improve the organisation and its impact on the world. I discuss sustainability more in chapter 11.

- **Board and risk committees.** As I said above, the CRO should have a direct line to the board and risk committees, consisting of independent directors for reporting and escalation. Independent directors bring valuable perspective and experience to the CRO; they can help to identify an area of risk that is not being given enough attention or come up with mitigants, approaches and solutions that they have seen used elsewhere. Establishing the right governance and oversight is a critical function for the CRO, and I discuss this in Chapter 13.

In Figure 1.2 below, I've summarised the key risk areas for each executive role outlined above. Note that risks can often apply across multiple areas.

| Role | Key risks covered |
|---|---|
| CEO | Strategic risk |
| COO | All operational risks, change management risk, model risk, physical security risk, supplier risk, financial crime risk, transaction processing risk |
| CCO/CRO | Conduct risk and risks related to misalignment of incentives |
| CTO / CISO | Information security risk, cybersecurity risk, business continuity |
| CPO (Product) | Product risks (product not meeting customer expectations, poor design, poor implementation, etc.) |
| CFO | Capital and liquidity risk, credit and counterparty risk, market risk, financial reporting risk, fraud risk, financial crime risk, model risk |
| CPO (People) | People risk, conduct risk |

| | |
|---|---|
| CMO | Conduct risk |
| CLO | Regulatory risk, litigation risk |

Figure 1.2 Key risk areas for each executive role.

The role of the CRO is to help each of these executives understand their myriad business and risk responsibilities, and to balance the pursuit of growth with good risk management.

## Summary

It may seem as if there is a long list of attributes and considerations for the CRO role – and there is! However, as with the COO, few people come into their first role "fully formed". With research and support, learning continues on the job. In any case, the external environment is changing so rapidly that new risks appear all the time which require new approaches, and so the role and the scope of activity will always evolve. Having a good team around you, an open mindset, analytical skills, the ability to work through complex problems without fear and a desire to collaborate without ego will allow a prospective CRO to tackle most issues effectively.

> *"It is important to note that you do not need to be strong in every single factor—indeed, successful leaders are rarely well-rounded in all areas. Instead, they will have exceptional areas of talent, usually offset with some significant development needs. The goal for a risk leader is to develop a foundational level of capability in the most important areas, play to their distinctive strengths, be aware of development gaps and ensure that there are measures in place to compensate for them."* [14]

# SECTION ONE - THE FOUNDATIONS

# Chapter 2

## The importance of a risk-aware culture

*"Creating or shaping a more risk-aware culture is… potentially the greatest value a risk function can bring to the table in terms of preparing their organization for the challenges of uncertain and fast-changing environments."* [15]

If, as Edgar Schein defines it, culture is *"a system of shared assumptions, values and beliefs"*, how do culture and risk affect each other? We know that culture guides staff behaviour more than anything else – more than rules and even, at times, more than their own personalities. Culture is the most powerful influencer of behaviour in the workplace and therefore must be considered first when it comes to risk.

*"An organisation's culture, and by extension, its risk culture, is both a source of strength and weakness when it comes to the management of Operational Risk."* [16]

This means that, without a suitably attuned risk culture, all your work on risk frameworks, policies and procedures will fail to take root in the organisation. Winning staff hearts and minds and ensuring a risk-aware culture permeates the organisation will, on the other hand, amplify all your other efforts.

Regulators see this too. In 2014, the Financial Stability Board (FSB) released a framework for assessing risk culture, saying:

*"A sound risk culture consistently supports appropriate risk awareness, behaviours and judgements about risk-taking within a strong risk governance framework. A sound risk culture bolsters effective risk management, promotes sound risk-taking, and ensures that emerging risks or risk-taking activities beyond the institution's risk appetite are recognised, assessed, escalated and addressed in a timely manner."* [17]

## What is risk culture?

We can see the importance of a sound risk culture, but what is it exactly? The Institute of Risk Management (IRM) defines culture as arising from repeated *"behaviour of the group"*, which in turn is shaped by their underlying *"attitudes"*. This culture then influences the behaviour and attitudes of members, creating a cycle that feeds on itself. Taking this framework and applying it to risk culture, we see that:

- *Risk attitude is "the chosen position adopted by an individual or group towards risk, influenced by risk perception".*
- *Risk behaviour comprises external, observable risk-related actions, including risk-based decision-making, risk processes, risk communications, etc.*
- *Risk culture is "the values, beliefs, knowledge and understanding about risk, shared by a group of people with a common purpose".* [18]

As a new or aspiring CRO, take time to look at the behaviours and attitudes in the organisation towards risk – is it a maverick culture, with disdain for rules and regulations? Or respectful and considerate? Has the risk pendulum swung too far, such that the organisation is afraid to take any risk at all? What has happened in the past when faced with difficult decisions – how did management address the problem? These all give you an indication of attitude to risk.

The IRM designed a Risk Culture Aspects Model with eight components, grouped into four themes.[19] It is designed to categorise and define the key drivers of risk culture so that a company can identify their own gaps, problems and areas for improvement. It's a useful framework for you to use to evaluate culture.

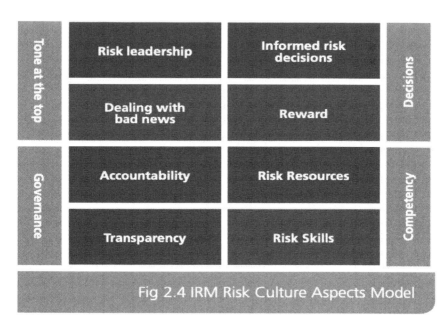

Figure 2.1 The IRM's Risk Culture Aspects Model

Let's look at the four themes in more detail.

- **Tone at the top** deals with how leaders exemplify their attitude to risk and also how they have been seen to deal with bad news in the past. Do they welcome transparency and openness, or did they "shoot the messenger" in the past? These totemic actions by management are remembered by staff and inform future behaviour.

- **Governance** looks at how clearly accountability for risk is defined and whether risk information is available and shared transparently. Also, how strong is the voice of independent bodies such as regulators and the board?
- **Competency** refers to the ability and talent of the risk resources in the organisation and the extent to which risk knowledge and skills are disseminated. Is the organisation risk-enabled?
- Finally, **Decisions** looks at the rigour behind the decisions that are taken in the organisation and whether the right behaviours get rewarded.

## How to assess the risk culture of your organisation

The IRM and Protiviti created a comprehensive source of risk culture resources in which they offer guidance on how to evaluate your own risk culture at the organisation, team and individual level.[20] In an article by Jim DeLoach of Protiviti, he recommends assessing the organisation via self-assessment techniques, internal surveys and focus groups, looking at topics such as tone, reinforcement, internal and external environment and subcultures.[21]

As culture starts at the top, it is helpful to look to the board and executive team first. You can start by exploring attitudes to risk, including the organisation's "stories" that have shaped and serve to exemplify the historic risk culture. You can also explore, with both teams and individuals, how they feel risk has been handled and why. Cross-functional, small in-person workshops are a great way to take the pulse. In addition, online survey tools, such as

OfficeVibe and Mentimeter, are useful low-impact ways to hear from the organisation and offer rapid insights.

## How to build a risk-aware culture

Once you have assessed the risk culture of the company, how can you as CRO influence leadership to shape that culture towards risk awareness? There are, of course, informal methods. You could work with your executive team to follow up the assessment above with targeted interventions, coaching and workshops to address areas of weakness. However, you can also take a more structured approach, using frameworks that set out a specific pathway. In this chapter, I reference;

- The Financial Stability Board's (FSB) Framework for Assessing Risk Culture;
- Edgar Schein's 12 Steps for Culture Change

Plus a couple of other problem-solving frameworks. These can be used, depending on the circumstances, to help you assess weak areas and drive improvement.

### The FSB's Framework for Assessing Risk Culture

A good place to start in setting the desired culture is looking at the guidance created by the FSB, entitled: 'Guidance on Supervisory Interaction with Financial Institutions on Risk Culture'. They outline four factors that will help to shape and improve the risk culture: *Tone from the top*, *Accountability*, *Effective communication and challenge* and *Incentives*. Below, I'll go through each and outline what they mean in practice.

### Tone from the top

- **Leading by example.** Any assessment of culture, and any efforts to reform it, must start at the top of the organisation, where those in power set the tone. Are the board and executives explicit about risk management? Do they have a view that is clearly expressed? Do their actions mirror their words? A *"lack of management or board direction"* was identified by 41% of respondents as the biggest challenge for risk culture development.[22] Addressing risk head-on, having a clear point of view on what risks the organisation will, and will not, take and repeating it regularly is a good place to start.

- **Ensuring common understanding and awareness of risk throughout the organisation.** Next, management must take steps to ensure that their agreed-upon risk view is cascaded, reliably and consistently, throughout the organisation and that staff at all levels are hearing the same messages. Is the risk framework embedded in the organisation? Do the processes and systems support the risk view? Is decision-making referencing the agreed risk appetite? Management and boards should be ensuring this is happening. As the US National Association of Corporate Directors says, *"Boards should monitor the tone at the bottom"* in order to gain insight into how well the risk strategy is understood.[23]

- **Learning from past experiences.** Often, the differentiator between success and failure is not whether risk events happen or not – they do – but in how the organisation responds. If it is learning, incrementally, from each thing that goes wrong, building maturity and corporate knowledge, then it is growing and evolving.

One very powerful tool I have observed is for staff to hear directly from the front line when something has gone wrong. In one of my roles, nothing was more effective at stopping the internal arguing than to hear compelling testimony about how an issue had caused problems for a customer. It was a powerful way to bring people back to why we were there in the first place and to overcome internal frustrations in order to focus on problem-solving.

- **The importance of a "no-blame" culture.** In order to embrace learning and recognise weaknesses before they occur, people must feel able to raise issues without fear of reprisal. A culture of openness and transparency is essential to create a feeling of psychological safety.

This has been a particular issue in the health services area where, previously, more junior staff may have felt unable to call out a problem in front of a more senior doctor, consultant or registrar. In the UK, fear of authority in the NHS historically fostered a defensive culture that closed down discussion of mistakes. However, in recent years they have done a lot to promote a "no-blame" culture of "intelligent transparency", encouraging medical professionals to speak up when something looks wrong and giving them credit for that during tribunals, with resulting improvements in patient safety and outcomes.[24]

**Accountability**

- **Ownership of risk.** Responsibilities for risk management must be clearly assigned and visibly "owned", by first-line business functions. How articulate are those leaders in describing these risks, and how they will be managed? If the relevant executives are able to show strong leadership in this way, employees will be able to easily identify these risks and quickly report them to the correct party. It will provide a reassuring structure within which risks cannot be swept under the carpet or ignored.

*"Examples of ethical leadership will foster trust and thus reduce fears, minimize the feeling of vulnerability, and, in general, lower the level of stress that might be caused by facing the uncertainty."*[25]

- **Escalation processes.** When things go wrong, there must be clear escalation protocols in place. When a system goes down, an office suffers damage, or a PR issue erupts, people need to know who to contact – fast. They need to be adequately supported by systems that are tested and evidenced as working. Has management invested the time in ensuring these protocols are robust?
- **Clear consequences.** When something does go wrong and a person takes an action that is not in line with the organisation's risk appetite, values or culture, the organisation needs to see that there are consequences. This doesn't mean "hanging people out to dry" or finding the easiest scapegoat. It does mean being transparent when things go wrong, learning from the event and, where misconduct has occurred, taking swift and decisive action.

*Effective communication and challenge*
- **Openness to alternative views.** The organisation's openness to alternative views from employees, other companies or outside bodies demonstrates its willingness to be held accountable if it has made a mistake. If leadership ignore or shut out any and all challenges to their perspective then it will be hard for them to learn and grow from failures. How willing is the organisation to engage in debate? Is it open to hearing dissenting voices? Does it encourage people to speak up if they are uncomfortable or is challenge viewed as disloyalty?

*"As with all aspects of good governance, the effectiveness of risk management depends on the individuals responsible for operating the systems put in place. Our risk culture must embrace openness, support transparency, welcome constructive challenge and promote collaboration, consultation and cooperation. We must invite scrutiny and embrace expertise to inform decision-making. We must also invest in the necessary capabilities and seek to continually learn from experience."[26]*

- **Respect for risk functions.** I have often said that organisations get the risk professionals they deserve. Those who respect the risk profession and its independence, listen to their risk managers, promote and develop their risk staff and give priority to risk topics will typically have the most talented and capable risk managers because these are attractive places for them to work. Those who pay lip service to risk will typically attract only the risk professionals who don't have a lot of options – a bad outcome for all.

## Incentives

- **Including risk in performance rewards.** In organisations where there are rewards for performance, it's good practice to explicitly highlight risk as a key component. Holistic performance and reward assessment should therefore take into account:

  1. whether the person achieved their business objectives;
  2. how they went about achieving them, i.e. the values and behaviours they espoused; and
  3. their attitude towards risk: whether they managed risk, adhered to guidelines, did their risk training, called out issues, helped drive improvement, etc.

This actively shows employees that the organisation takes risk seriously and is willing to align incentives to its risk environment.

- **Taking account of risk behaviour when planning promotions.** Does the organisation place value on risk management capabilities when looking at who to promote? Is there an acknowledged balance between doing the right thing and generating revenues and profits? Are the prospects for progression within risk management as likely and attractive as those in the front office?
- **Training and professional development in risk.** Are all employees being trained in risk management theory and practice and how this can support the organisation? Is there job mobility between first-line roles and risk, to promote mutual understanding? Are risk employees properly trained and developed? These are all good steps to take to build a stronger risk culture.

*"A culture that is conducive to effective risk management encourages open and upward communication, sharing of knowledge and best practices, continuous process improvement and a strong commitment to ethical and responsible business behavior."*[27]

## Edgar Schein's 12 Steps for Culture Change

In Schein's work on culture, he identifies 12 mechanisms by which leaders embed their beliefs, values and assumptions within the organisation.[28] These are broken down into the most impactful methods that should be prioritised (primary) and other methods that will support these actions (secondary).[29]

Primary

1. What they pay attention to, measure and control regularly
2. How they react to critical incidents and organisational crises
3. How they allocate resources
4. Role modelling, teaching and coaching
5. How they allocate rewards and status
6. How they recruit, select, promote and excommunicate

Secondary

7. Organisational design and structure
8. Organisational systems and procedures
9. Rites and rituals of the organisation
10. Design of physical space, facades and buildings
11. Stories about important events and people
12. Formal statements of organisational philosophy, creeds and charters

The list above was written about culture generally, not risk culture. However, as you read, it becomes clear that each of these mechanisms can be deployed to build and strengthen a risk-aware culture. For example:

- Does the senior leadership team (and not just the CRO) talk about risk, resilience and putting the customer first?
- Do they reward those who go the extra mile to test, quality assure and challenge?
- Is the risk career path an attractive one, or is it difficult to get recognised, paid and promoted?
- How is bad behaviour dealt with?
- Does the organisation celebrate and highlight examples where eagle-eyed staff spotted a risk and escalated it?

These actions by all the leadership team are what staff notice and respond do. Taking these 12 factors and assessing where the organisation is vs. where it would like to be can form the basis of a culture-change plan. This demonstrates that culture can be changed but only with clear and strong intent from leadership.

## Other problem-solving approaches

As well as top-down communication, it can be helpful to empower staff with actionable daily values and tools for decision-making when confronted with ethical dilemmas that may include risk. The Project Management Institute recognised the benefit of guidance for its practitioners, and the resulting framework offers a five-step approach when faced with an ethical challenge:[30]

1. **Assessment:** Make sure you have all the facts about the ethical dilemma.
2. **Alternatives:** Consider your options.
3. **Analysis:** Identify your candidate decision (your preferred choice from the range of options) and assess its validity.
4. **Application:** Apply ethical principles, including responsibility, respect, fairness and honesty, to your candidate decision.
5. **Action:** Make a decision. If you are comfortable, then proceed. If not, then reperform the exercise until you can get comfortable.

Finally, the DMAIC is a five-phase approach, taken from Lean Six-Sigma; it helps with problem solving and decision-making.[31] The five steps are; Define, Measure, Analyse, Improve and Control. It's particularly good for getting to the root of undefined problems.

## Summary

Arguably your more important task as a CRO is promoting a risk-aware culture, both directly in your actions, and by influencing the attitude and approach of everyone in the organisation, from leadership downwards. While this can be extremely difficult, holding a mirror up to the corporate culture and taking confident and committed steps to transform or strengthen it is the key to successful risk management.

> *"It is possible for an organisation to drive change in its risk culture. This requires a clear understanding of the current culture and the desired 'target' culture. It requires recognition that this is a major change programme and requires discipline to see it through. The culture change should be treated as a change management project in its own right, with appropriate allocation of board time and resources."*[32]

With a solid grounding and a plan in place to address culture, you now need to assess the organisation's strategy and how it will interact with risk.

# Chapter 3

*Risk and organisational strategy*

Risk and organisational strategy are inextricably linked and need to be considered alongside one another. When developing a risk framework, you should always begin with an awareness of the organisation's strategic objectives. Risk is, after all, uncertainty that has the potential to affect (positively or negatively) the attainment of these objectives. As stated in ISO31000 (the ISO's standards on risk management), risk is *"uncertainty relating to organisational outcomes"*.[33]

In addition, there is also the element of "strategic risk" to be considered – the risk that the organisation's strategy is the wrong one, or is not well-executed, leading to the potential for an organisation's products or services (and indeed the organisation itself) becoming redundant. We discuss this risk more in Chapter 6.

Risk management should feed into organisational strategy as much as strategy feeds into risk management. As the NHS risk management framework says: *"A risk management strategy has a key role to play in providing the strategic context within which detailed capital and revenue investment plans and business cases can be developed."* [34]

*"Unmanaged risk costs unbudgeted money."[35]*

That most basic tool of strategy, the SWOT analysis, has the concept of risk built into it. Opportunities and threats, two of the four factors that are analysed within this framework, are simply alternative words for upside and downside risks. When conducting a SWOT analysis, management is asking itself, "What strengths do we have that we can use to exploit opportunities?" and, "What weaknesses do we have that can be exposed by threats?". They then design a risk-aware strategy to make the most of the opportunities available and try to build capability to protect, or shore up, their weak areas.

## Official risk frameworks and the link with strategy

As mentioned, ISO31000 provides a framework for managing risk which highlights the link with organisational strategy. The 2018 update provides *"more strategic guidance"* than its predecessor and *"places more emphasis on both the involvement of senior management and the integration of risk management into the organization"*.[36] The standard now also recommends that *"risk management be part of the organization's structure, processes, objectives, strategy and activities"*.[37] This provides endorsement of the fact that risk and strategy need to be considered alongside one another. The eight principles of ISO31000 state that:

1. Risk management is an integral part of all organisational activities;
2. A structured and comprehensive approach is required;
3. The framework and processes should be customised to the organisation and appropriate for the context;
4. Stakeholders should be involved in an appropriate and timely way;
5. Risk management anticipates, detects, acknowledges and responds to changes;

6. Risk management factors in limitations of available information;

7. Human and cultural factors need to be considered in risk management; and

8. Risk management must be continually improved via learning and experience.[38]

## What are the strategic components of a risk framework?

So, how do we begin to develop a risk framework from a strategic perspective? As we can see, organisational strategy and risk management rely heavily on one another. Let's consider what questions we seek to answer when developing organisational strategy as a starting point.

- What is our mission?
- What does success look like?
- What is it that we do better than anyone else?
- What are our goals?
- How will we get there?
- What markets, channels and product spaces do we need to be in?
- Who do we need to partner with, acquire and divest?
- What could throw us off course?

Being effective in your CRO role requires a fundamental understanding of the above – take the time to interrogate the organisation's strategy, ideally before you start in the role. Your role will be to extend the answers to the above and develop the risk context around them, to establish:

- What the organisation is truly trying to achieve;
- What could happen to impact those objectives, both positively

and negatively;
- How likely are those events to happen, and what would the impact be?
- How the organisation can set itself up to mitigate risk;
- What strategies will be needed to avoid, protect and defend against or mitigate those events happening?

Getting time with the executive team, staff and board to develop a sound, shared understanding of strategy and risk is time well spent and will make all the downstream work easier.

## The McKinsey 7-S model: The strategic foundations of a risk framework

Another useful model to consider risk is the 7-S model, developed by former McKinsey consultants Thomas J. Peters and Robert H. Waterman. It's a very useful way of breaking down the components of a successful organisational strategy, and it has just as much relevance when building a risk framework, as the two go hand in hand. Let's consider each of the seven components in turn.

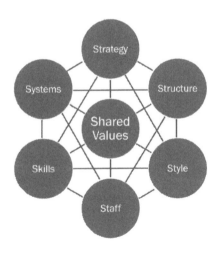

Figure 3.1 The McKinsey 7-S Model

## Strategy

The risk strategy must support the overall organisational strategy, including the brand and customer proposition. As I've said, no venture is without risk. The risk strategy can be used to place limits on how far the organisation goes in pursuit of its goals. Choosing which products or services to sell, how to market them, in which markets and channels, all should be done by balancing the benefits with the risks involved.

## Structure

The structure of the organisation can be leveraged to manage risk. Proper allocation of responsibilities, segregation of duties and the avoidance of conflicts of interest, as well as governance and oversight arrangements, ensure the organisation is set up to be resilient. The identification of the three lines of defence, and clear accountabilities, all contribute to the risk strategy – and to the attainment of organisational goals.

## Systems

A well-managed technology platform, with genuine built-in resilience, security and monitoring, supports the organisation's mission as well as its risk objectives. In addition, the organisation must give thought to the systems, data and intelligence it needs to predict, identify, mitigate and manage risks. Well-designed processes are also a part of good systems. We discuss technology risk in Chapter 8.

## Staff

The composition and skill sets of the staff, the culture that is engendered, their training and development and their goals and motivations all contribute to the organisation's resilience to risk. In addition, the composition of the risk team, their seniority, incentives and reinforcement and the attention they receive from management can all impact on the organisation's strength. We discuss people risk in Chapter 7.

## Style

An organisation's style and brand also reference risk, either implicitly or explicitly. For example, Virgin Airlines built its brand on its pioneering founder, Richard Branson, who even wrote a book called *Screw It, Let's Do It.* Ryanair built a reputation that reset (i.e. lowered!) customer expectations for what they could expect to get "for free" as part of the ticket they bought. In contrast, more traditional airline carriers such as British Airways perhaps strive for a more "cocooning" customer experience that also leverages the national brand. This style influences and pervades these organisations and informs the culture, which includes attitude towards risk.

## Skills

How well-understood is risk by all staff? How clear are they on the organisation's unique selling points? How robust is their testing and modelling? How well do they understand their customers? How well-trained are they to execute their roles? A CRO can do a lot to raise the level of risk-awareness in the organisation and to place emphasis on strong processes and tools to enhance risk management. A staffing plan that emphasises hiring the right people, developing them, rewarding the right behaviours and building up corporate knowledge is building resilience to risk.

## Superordinate goals

We've said that risk is the uncertainty that could affect the achievement of the organisation's goals. The risk strategy starts with an understanding of what the organisation wants to achieve, whether it's growth, profitability, etc., and what key events could thwart those aims. The superordinate goals are the reason why the organisation exists. Take, for example, Elon Musk's assertion that "… Twitter serves as the de facto public town square". He then went on to say that, "failing to adhere to free speech principles fundamentally undermines democracy".[39] This gave us a clue as to his intentions, at time of writing, for the company and the risks he may be willing to take, or not take.

## Stakeholders

Personally, I would also add another "s" for stakeholders. Stakeholder mapping is a critical piece of risk management. It's important to consider all stakeholders and identify their concerns and agendas. Key stakeholders could include the following:

- Customers;
- Employees;
- Suppliers;
- Regulators;
- Investors;
- Shareholders;
- Media;
- Government; and
- the Public.

Developing a strong understanding of, and relationship with, your stakeholder groups allows you and the organisation to anticipate where problems may occur and hopefully pre-empt unpleasant surprises.

## Summary

This chapter has focused on strategy and risk and how the two are inextricably linked. Organisational strategy and risk management inform and support one another – they are symbiotic. Starting with this understanding, we are able to build a risk framework using the foundation of common strategic objectives and analysis. Once we have the strategy in place, we then need to make sure it's alive and embedded in the organisation – we have to think about execution.

# Chapter 4

*Risk and execution*

The best risk framework in the world is worthless if not supported by solid execution. The skill of the CRO lies in not only setting out the vision for the risk framework, but in turning it into understandable, easy to access day-to-day operations.

> *"The presence of an Operational Risk Management Framework is a necessary part of Operational Risk Management, but is rarely adequate in isolation… Organisations must ensure that the ORMF is embedded in day-to-day business activities and decisions."*[40]

## Using the risk framework in practice

A theoretical risk framework that doesn't inform an organisation's actions is useless.

It's a sad fact that many of the risk frameworks in organisations today are purely tick-box exercises. They are updated periodically and then put back on the shelf. They're not used actively and not checked against reality. They don't inform decisions. As risks evolve and change over time, it's also likely that they're out of date and incorrect. It's a terrible waste of management time and a missed opportunity to enrich decision-making. It's imperative that the theoretical risk exercise meets with reality, and as CRO, you play a pivotal role in bringing it all to life. One way to do this is by regularly juxtaposing what people think the situation is with the reality that is taking place. For example, where are risks actually occurring vs. where did management think they would occur? What are the root causes of recent incidents and losses, and do they reflect a faulty framework or a lack of risk awareness?

Below is a list of useful reflection points that will help you to assess this gap between theoretical risk frameworks and what is happening on the ground:

- If a large proportion of risk events are stemming from one root cause but that isn't recognised by management in their self-assessment, then perhaps there is a blind spot that needs to be looked at. Calling out those clusters of risk events will allow you to address the perception gap that exists.
- Conversely, if something is recognised as a very high likelihood risk, expected to occur semi-frequently, but it hasn't taken place in that time, you can question whether it's as big a risk as was previously thought. Did the organisation just get lucky? Or is there a chance that the organisation has "gold-plated" the controls in this space, perhaps to excess, hampering their ability to move?
- Often, risk teams may raise a risk but the first-line manager in the area seems relatively unconcerned about it occurring. When pressed, the manager reels off a list of reasons why they think it's not such a big deal. This is great - they are actually listing a set of compensating controls and mitigants, they just never recognised them as such. A skilled risk manager can draw these insights out and strengthen the risk analysis in doing so. As long as those compensating factors

are accurate and thorough, they can be taken into account and the risk level reduced as appropriate.

- Where the organisation has areas of genuine exposure, when they could lose real money or have real safety issues, have these been recognised and rigorously controlled across systems, processes and people? This is where you want the resources of the organisation to be deployed.

- How many of the risk events that actually materialised were recognised as risks before they occurred? Could they and should they have been foreseen? This tells you a lot about organisational self-awareness and how reliable the first line's self-assessments are.

- Where there are weaknesses identified by one department, could they be compounded by weaknesses elsewhere to create a true vulnerability for the organisation? An example would be a system's weakness compounded by a staff shortage and poor training. Compounded risks such as these are often responsible for some of the biggest risk events. I discuss this problem in more detail in Chapter 16.

Let's consider an example, below, where the checks and balances of a risk framework seemed to be absent in the process of day-to-day product development.

## Case study: Cyberpunk 2077

- In January 2021, CEO of CD Projekt, Marcin Iwinski, took responsibility for the *"disastrous rollout"* of a new game, Cyberpunk 2077. He acknowledged that the game *"did not meet the quality standard we wanted to meet"*.[41]

- Cyberpunk 2077 was an ambitious project to begin with. The virtual "city" in which the game is set was loaded with more content than previous versions. This was going to be an issue for older generation consoles.

- In addition, there was a lot of new technology and techniques involved – the game was experienced by gamers in the first person and not viewed as a third person.
- There was also a lot of foundational infrastructure build taking place at the same time as the development of the front-end user experience. *"One member of the team compared the process to trying to drive a train while the tracks are being laid in front of you at the same time."*
- Testing didn't uncover the issues, or if it did, there wasn't time to fix them.
- Warnings from staff were not heeded, with the company pursuing cycle after cycle of "crash work" where staff were regularly asked to work over and above normal hours to try to complete the project. When subsequently interviewed, employees talked about *"a development process marred by unchecked ambition, poor planning and technical shortcomings"*.
- The eagerly anticipated game suffered delays and glitches on PCs, Xboxes and PlayStations, eventually leading to the game being withdrawn and refunds offered to customers.
- The impact was a 30% drop in the Polish company's share price between December and January 2021, and even speculation that CD Projekt could be sold off.[42]

The above case study illustrates how it's often a collection of risks that contribute, jointly, to a risk event materialising. When viewed in hindsight, it would appear that there were numerous warning signs that could have been heeded. Any one of them could have triggered a stand-back or pause, and prevented a larger, more visible issue down the line.

## Embedding risk assessment through all stages of a project

So, how can we avoid this sort of situation when running projects, whether it's delivering software or launching a new product? How can we ensure that risk management is not just a box to be checked but that it is alive and embedded into each step of the decision-making process? Below are some appropriate considerations that will flag issues at the correct time, allowing resolution before it's too late.

- **Inception of a product/project/venture**. Is this the right product for the time and the customer base? Is it the best use of the organisation's resources? Do we have enough data to be comfortable that this is what our customers want? Will regulators look favourably on the product? Is it buildable? Is it sustainable? Does it link to the medium-term strategy? Is it where the market is moving?
- **Design phase**. Is the product or service offering / new division being built to last? Is the right technology architecture in place? In engineering, are the right languages, container solutions and environment choices being made? Can we road-test the concept with customers, even now? Testing can never start soon enough – the consumer product Moma came about from its inventor creating bircher muesli at home, putting it in plastic pots and handing it out for free in Waterloo station, in return for feedback.
- **Development**. Does the company have a strong process for development and testing? In coding, is the code properly structured, adequately commented and signposted? Are the right check-in and check-out procedures in place? Is there peer review in place? What are the controls before

new code is checked in? DevSecOps is an approach in which security and testing are done at the same time as coding, by the developer. Done correctly, it's a great way of building in security and quality at the outset.

- **Testing**. Even if rigorous unit testing has been built in at the development stage, ensure the team does not neglect the more holistic end-to-end testing and user acceptance testing stages. This ensures that the user experience is what was really intended, and that the product or service (including all the associated systems and processes) works as a whole. It also puts the product in the hands of users, which often yields tons of unexpected results and insights.

- **Rollout (software)**. If you work in an agile development environment, the chances are that code deployment is happening regularly, perhaps several times a day. Modern environments make the code check-in and deployment steps very smooth and automated. Older environments will have a longer set of steps to go through to deploy new code from the build into the live environment.

- **Rollout (customers).** Whose role is it to ensure the new product or service offering lands well in the hands of customers? Are all stakeholders involved? Have all aspects such as after-sales care, operations and customer services been considered?

- **Review**. This is critical to the learning process, as it captures the experiences which can feed into future decision-making. How is the new product being used? Are there analytics in place to tell us how customers are enjoying the new product or feature? Are there any glitches in the experience? What is the plan for gathering rapid feedback in the early days of the launch, and how is this information being used?

If done well, all of the above steps and considerations should be a natural part of the product development process. They should feel seamless and intuitive, with quality built in at each stage rather than inspected out. When product problems occur, good organisations resist the understandable temptation to add layers of inspection on top. Instead, go back to the core of the process and work with your engineering and operations teams to make it excellent from the inside out.

## Creating a new product approval process

If your organisation is innovating at all, you will need a mechanism for assessing new products and ventures and ensuring they are fit for purpose to avoid unnecessary risk. For example, do you want a process to check whether it will fit customer needs? If regulated, will the product stand up to the regulations? Can it be supported by operations and customer service? Has it been rigorously tested?

A robust new product-approval process will address these issues, ensuring that the product is set up for success. The purpose of new product approval is to allow internal stakeholders a chance to assess the product and ensure it's robust. All affected parties should have a chance to put forward any conditions they need to be fulfilled in order to make the launch a success. The kind of input you usually see from different business functions are as follows:

-   **Legal and compliance.** Is the wording in the product documentation correct and appropriate? Is the product being promoted fairly and correctly? (For example, in financial services, financial promotion requirements say that the product must be *"fair, accurate and not misleading")*. Does it meet all the legal requirements in the markets in which it will be sold?

- **Operations.** Can the product be built to work consistently? Can it be supported post-sale? Have the supporting processes been considered in full? Unnecessarily complex product design can cause severe downstream problems for the teams that have to support the product for maybe years later.
- **Customer services**. Is the product well-explained? Is the customer journey clear? Are there FAQs to support and inform customers? Have the CS team had the chance to vet and understand the product, and ensure they in turn can explain and support it to customers?
- **Engineering**. Can the product be built efficiently and sustainability? Has it been defined to the right level of precision? Does it make sense? If a technical product, are the data and logic requirements known and achievable?
- **Marketing**. Does the marketing team have enough information to be able to promote the product effectively? Are its attributes clear? Is the target customer group identified? What is the cost of acquisition of each customer? What's the lifetime value of the product (i.e. how much money will it make the organisation over its lifetime)?

Bear in mind, particularly in financial services, that it's important to consider the complexity of the product being offered vs. the level of sophistication of the client. If your organisation is viewed as promoting overly complex products to an unskilled public, the regulators and courts will likely find against you. We discuss this in more detail in the conduct risk section in Chapter 7.

## Involving risk in change management

Change inevitably brings risk. However, it's worth pointing out that lack of change, stasis and hubris can be just as risky to an organisation! Still, just as the majority of car accidents take place at road junctions, so it is that change – whether at the top level (acquisition, merger, divestment), at company level (new markets, team changes) or even at the transactional level (new releases, product launches, change of process) – creates risky moments in the organisation, and we benefit from a framework to assess the risks.

Having your risk professionals embedded in the team that is working on the change from the outset should allow for proper consideration of the risks and mitigants. Some organisations bring in teams such as risk and legal at the very last minute to "bless" the final product on the eve of launch, which rarely results in success or a good experience. In this situation, the risk and legal teams feel as if they've been put in an impossible position, with only the option of a binary "yes" or "no" answer to the product instead of the opportunity to make it better along the way. If it's a "no", the change team feel as if the risk team is just putting up blockers rather than helping them to solve the problem, and thus will be even less likely to involve them early on the next time. This is a common cycle that needs to be broken through early intervention, involving the right people and by risk and legal taking a more collaborative and solutions-focused approach.

## Summary

We've set a strong, risk-aware culture and now we have risk aligned with strategy. We've ensured that risk management is grounded in reality and that we're supporting organisational execution and change. It's time to get into the core of the risk management framework – assessing our key risks and identifying how to manage them.

# SECTION TWO – THE TECHNICAL AREAS

# Chapter 5

*Building your risk framework*

Having covered the pillars of culture, strategy and execution and their relationship with risk, we now move to the core business of the CRO – risk management. Here, we get into the core content of the risk framework itself. This is where we figure out what our key risks are and decide how much risk we're willing to take on board in pursuit of our organisational objectives. Once we've done that, we compare our current risk situation vs. what we want it to be. If all our risks are operating within our risk appetite, then great! However, if they are not, we have to decide what treatments we're going to prescribe. First, we will revisit the risk framework in more detail.

## The benefits of a risk framework

As we've seen in the previous chapters, there are obvious benefits to having a formal risk framework. The NHS lists the following benefits:

- Systematic decision-making;
- A clear hierarchy of risks;

- Improved understanding of the nature of risks;
- Management and staff ownership of risk issues;
- Improved morale and productivity; and
- Maintaining a safe environment for patients (or customers) and staff.

Beyond the simple risk framework is the concept of enterprise-wide risk management (EWRM or ERM) – a more holistic approach to risk strategy. ERM recognises that the differing risks an organisation encounters are interrelated and should be considered collectively in order to get an accurate view of overall risk. In practice, this usually means considering risks such as market risk, credit risk and operational risk together. However your organisation is managed, and however far your remit as CRO goes, it makes good sense to ensure that your risk committee pulls all of these risks together in one place for consideration.

## Using standards in your risk framework

There are several recognised risk standards that the CRO can refer to when examining (or, indeed, establishing) their risk framework. These include:

- ISO 31000 (2018), International Standards Organization;
- The COSO ERM "cube" (2004), COSO;
- The IRM standard (2002), Institute of Risk Management;[44]
- The Sarbanes-Oxley Act (2002);
- The UK Corporate Governance Code (2018);
- FRC guidelines; and
- The "Orange Book", UK Government.

ISO 31000 is the industry standard for enterprise risk management and is a good place to start when creating the foundation of your strategy.

It outlines the four components of the risk professional's role: planning and designing, implementing and benchmarking, measuring and monitoring and learning and reporting. These four areas should be considered and outlined in detail in your risk framework. Below I have summarised what activities these areas should comprise.

**Planning and designing:** This includes writing the risk policy; setting the board mandate and commitment to risk management; defining the roles of the audit and risk committees, the executive team and the risk management team.

**Implementing and benchmarking**: Usually this entails performing risk assessments, reviews, analysis and horizon scanning, including looking at the external environment and other players for comparison to your own situation.

**Measuring and monitoring:** Recording and evaluating risks; evaluating the controls or mitigants that should reduce them; aggregating the impact of risk incidents and understanding why they occurred in order to avoid them in future.

**Learning and reporting:** Finally, this involves closing the loop; embedding a culture of ongoing learning and improvement so that the organisation's considerable investment in risk management pays off over time.

Once we have implemented the fundamentals of building a risk framework, let's consider the steps we need to take to develop a risk strategy that reflects the specific context of the organisation. The first step is to assess what your risks are and prioritise them in order of importance. You then need to set an appetite for those risks to take place. Finally, you must outline the strategies and processes for dealing with risks when they occur. As I've mentioned before, this is not about removing risk altogether. All enterprise is ultimately about taking a series of calculated and managed risks in pursuit of an organisational goal.

## Setting risk appetite

The IRM defines risk appetite as *"the amount of risk that an organisation is willing to take in order to achieve its strategic objectives"*.[45] Risk appetite is often thought of in terms of a monetary amount – how much can we lose doing this? That is, of course, an important consideration. However, there are other measures of risk appetite, such as the following:

- **Reputation and brand.** How much damage is the organisation willing to suffer in the eyes of the public and its customers?
- **Company impact.** How much disruption to its operations is it willing and able to sustain?
- **Legal and regulatory.** What appetite does it have for legal disputes or "sailing close to the wind" on regulatory issues, taking into account further financial risks beyond direct loss, such as those from fines and compensation.
- **Opportunity cost.** What is the opportunity cost of pursuing option A over option B? As we saw in the chapter on strategic risk, one of the most finite (and under-appreciated) resources that organisations have is management time and focus. By failing to exercise strategic discipline, failing to cull suboptimal projects or lines of business, management is draining its most precious resource. Does your organisation want to adopt a "try lots of things and fail fast" approach, or something more tightly controlled?

The appropriate level of risk appetite is usually proposed by senior management to the board, who review and sign off the upper limits of risk tolerance, in monetary, reputational, operational and legal/regulatory terms. This is, or should be, a non-trivial exercise, as this process provides the organisation with the freedom to operate, as long as they stay within defined limits. Overly simplistic statements, such as "the organisation has zero tolerance for disruption" are not helpful here. The risk statements need to be grounded in reality, and to discuss the trade-offs and costs of the risk levels chosen.

## Identifying risks

The first stage is identifying the risks that exist for your organisation. You need to be comprehensive to ensure, as far as possible, that no issues which could trip you up in the future are left unexplored. This is an opportunity as a new, or aspiring, CRO to pull key people in the organisation together and explore both the risks that are in plain sight, and the risks that are less obvious and need to be explored. Your board should also be an invaluable source of risk assessment, especially if your directors work across several different organisations and sectors.

How can you be comfortable that your organisation has considered the widest possible set of risks? Below are some methods for risk identification that should help ensure a comprehensive approach:

- **Horizon scanning and tracking emerging risk trends:** Looking to external sources to see what events are taking place in your industry, sector or in the risk space generally. Don't neglect the opportunity to compare yourself with others. Scanning news feeds and monitoring freely available risk intel is valuable. Third-party organisations such as Acin also allow you to benchmark yourself against others in your sector and identify where you have gaps, blind spots or where your controls are lagging behind those of your peers.

- **Keeping up to date with regulatory requirements and changes:** Monitoring the changes that your regulator is proposing and being sensitive to current areas of concern. It's sometimes possible to take an active influencing role here too.
- **Undertaking risk and control self-assessments:** Internal assessments of the state of your current control environment. I discuss these in Chapter 12.
- **Analysing internal loss data:** Where has the organisation suffered loss in the past?
- **Benchmarking and analysis of external data:** What trends can you glean from how others in your sector are managing a particular issue?
- **Scenario analysis:** Answering the "What would happen if…?" questions.
- **Considering key risk indicators (KRIs):** E.g. staffing trends, trade volumes, new account volumes, product approvals and customer complaints.
- **Reviewing industry standards and best practice:** What is considered the norm in your sector? Consultancies are often a rich source of data here.

## Detecting and prioritising key risks

Once you have identified all of the risks to your organisation, you can use risk assessment to explore which of these are "key risks" i.e. which will have the greatest impact and the highest likelihood of occurring. These are the, usually no more than 20 or so, biggest risks that your organisation will face in the pursuit of its mission and objectives.

Risk assessment involves you identifying the impact on the organisation, usually across two spheres:

1) Impact if it happened.

It's important that management gauge the magnitude of the risk event if it occurred. The most obvious measure of risk is a loss, often measured in monetary terms. However, there are other considerations, such as regulatory implications, damage to the organisation's brand and reputation, impact on customers and other damage to the workings of the organisation.

2) Likelihood that it will happen.

You must initially assess the likelihood of a risk occurring on a standalone basis for an organisation such as yours – this is called *inherent risk*. After that, consider the current controls you have in place to prevent it happening and take these into account. This is called *residual risk*. If you have an excellent control framework in place, for example, the residual risk may drop so low that it ceases to be a key risk to the organisation.

### Inherent risk minus controls = residual risk

Now that you know what your key risks are, it's important to categorise and prioritise them to ensure you are well prepared when the most likely and impactful problems occur. Sometimes they are categorised into market, credit, liquidity and operational risks. Sometimes they are grouped into financial and non-financial risks. See the Appendix for a sample list. Either way, it's important that these are identified and the risk appetite for them is understood.

When thinking about the major risks facing an organisation, it struck me that there is a hierarchy that they occupy. The first and overarching risk is always strategic risk. If your organisation has got their overall strategy wrong or is failing to execute that strategy, then all the other risks are moot – the organisation won't be around for very long. Then you need to consider your people and the risks around them, then technology, before you think about the broader set of operational risks. As I looked at these, they naturally organised themselves into a pyramid of key risks, which I show below.

Figure 5.1 The pyramid of key risks.

Every organisation will have a slightly different set of risks that appear in the pyramid depending on their specific context. However, as it reflects a very standard hierarchy of risks, I will use this framework as a reference point in the ensuing chapters to analyse risks and associated controls.

## Creation of a risk register

A risk register is a useful way of pulling all the key risks together in a single place. At a minimum, a risk register should contain the following:

- Name;
- Description of the risk;
- Risk owner (the senior first-line manager in the organisation responsible for the risk);
- Perceived likelihood of occurring;
- Impact if it happened;
- Operational risk indicators (measures that test if the risk is occurring);
- Tolerances, limits and triggers for review;
- Number of historical risk events;
- Trend of risk (increasing/decreasing/static);
- Inherent risk (prior to controls);
- Controls to manage the risk;
- Control gaps (identifying where controls fall short);
- Action plan to address control gaps;
- Action plan owner; and
- Action plan due date.

This risk register becomes your anchor for how you track and report on risk on a regular basis. With this, you identify trends, emerging issues, improvements, setbacks, etc. Achieving a credible risk register that your executive peers understand and agree with is a key milestone as you set out your risk framework.

## Dealing with risks when they occur

Once you have identified all of the risks and organised them in priority order, your organisation needs a strategy to deal with them when problems occur. There is a broader range of control strategies to prevent and reduce risks than people naturally think about; we discuss these in more detail in Chapter 12. However, in terms of pure reaction to an event occurring, below are the key steps that a CRO should implement so their organisation can take effective action when required.

## Undertake risk event reporting

A critical process in risk management is the identification and reporting of risk events whenever they occur. This ensures the organisation responds quickly, learns from the risk event and becomes more resilient in the future; it is a critical element of "theory meeting reality". When capturing risk events, you want to include:

1. When the risk took place;
2. When it was detected;
3. How it was detected;
4. What happened;
5. What went wrong (there may have been more than one failure contributing to the event);
6. What the root cause was (see below for more detail on this point); and
7. What is being done to fix it, by who and by when.

It should not fall to the risk department to log and capture risks – one of the key mistakes risk departments make is not making their systems available and intuitive to business users at large. Everybody in the organisation should have the ability to log a risk event, and as it is (hopefully) not a frequent event, the risk system should be easy to access and intuitive to use.

In addition to the above mandatory information, there are further useful learning questions that can be asked. As part of risk event post-mortems, I have seen teams ask themselves: *"How did we get lucky?"* and *"How could it have been worse?"* Embracing an open, curious and questioning mindset in this way can yield truly valuable insights. The key is for it to be a safe learning space that is devoid of blame and which allows honest reflection.

Also, don't forget to acknowledge and discuss the risks that almost arose, often called "near misses". These are highly important to identify and learn from as they can prevent a much more serious event later on. Calling out near misses, in a no-blame environment, allows the organisation to learn about areas of weakness and resolve them before any loss occurs; they have been used with great success in financial services, the medical profession and the airline industry.

## Undertake root cause analysis

If an organisation is to learn from a risk event, it must understand the root causes. Not the symptoms, but the core reason why it went wrong. Common root causes ascribed to risk events include:

- Human error;
- Control design failure – the process was poorly designed to mitigate the risk in the first place;
- Control operation failure – the process was well designed but not executed as intended;
- Failure of testing and quality assurance; and
- Third-party failure.

There can be multiple root causes and the team affected should explore these to their conclusion. Exercises such as the "five whys" (an interrogative technique used to analyse the cause and effect of a problem) are often useful here. Independent challenge from the second line of defence is often useful too. So, for example, perhaps there was an error due to a staff member mis-keying an entry which caused a customer problem; why did they make the mistake? Were they trained? Had they worked a double shift that day and were tired? Was their manager supervising them adequately? Did they understand the significance of getting that field wrong? Was the user interface sufficiently clear? Investing time, in a safe space, with the right people, to interrogate what went wrong will give assurance that you can fix the problem in such a way that it won't recur.

## Create a risk action plan

Depending on the root cause(s) of a particular risk event, the team affected should agree the actions that will address and remediate the present risk, but more importantly, ensure it does not recur.

There are frequently multiple actions to address the root cause as risks events are often borne of a combination of factors. Some may take longer than others to address. So, to continue the example above, perhaps a customer situation needs to be put right immediately. Perhaps, when the dust settles, the front-line team goes on some refresher training. Perhaps the line manager needs a bit more support. Maybe the procedure document needs to be made more explicit or the text on the user screen improved. It is absolutely appropriate and normal to have a range of actions, both short and longer term, to close the risk to an acceptable level.

It's important to have accountability around the action plan and the CRO may need to prompt the accountable executive to set the tone for this: What are the actions, who is responsible and when will it be done by? How will we know whether it's done, and what measures will monitor the effectiveness of the new controls? Once the immediacy of the event has passed and been remediated, the momentum may be lost. The organisation needs the accountability and the tenacity, driven by the CRO (or ideally, the COO or other relevant executive), to drive through the necessary improvements.

## Incident response, business continuity management and resilience

A core part of the organisation's defence plan against risks is the rapid incident response plan. Whether the issue you've experienced is a software outage, a building emergency or a social media nightmare, the organisation should, as part of its planning, designate who will respond in the first instance, what the triage protocols are (i.e. deciding the immediate magnitude and urgency of the issue) and, if necessary, who gets woken up out of hours to deal with it. It should comprise rapid response plans on the technical, people and PR front. It should assign responsibility and empowerment, so there's no ambiguity about who has authority to act in pressured situations. Desk walkthroughs of these protocols, whereby you simulate a situation and have teams work through what they would do, are very effective at focusing the mind and getting people to implement improvements to their plans.

Business continuity management (BCM) has in recent years yielded to a focus on operational resilience. This is for a number of reasons; the Covid pandemic taught us that there are new levels of disruption to manage, which are hard to predict. In addition, the advent of cloud computing has made some aspects of traditional BCM (systems failover, hot sites, alternative office space) less relevant than they were before.

The more modern focus has been on "operational resilience", defined by KPMG[46] as "the ability to deliver critical operations in the face of disruption". This is a more foundational principle, and speaks just as much to the strategy, people management, systems and supply chain of the organisation, as it does to backup, recovery and restore procedures.

BCM and operational resilience are whole subjects in themselves. ISO 22300[47] covers security and resilience requirements. On the BCM front, it's still relevant and necessary to perform the following tasks:

- Business Impact Analysis (BIA) to map and understand your key processes;
- Triaging and prioritising key processes according to how quickly you need them back;
- Devising strategies for recovery from an event and documenting in a Business Continuity Plan;
- Periodic testing and walkthroughs;
- Ongoing horizon scanning for new potential events.

On the operational resilience front, I recommend taking a more expansive, questioning, cross-functional view, looking at how to build inherent resilience and redundancy into the organisational design. This includes looking at:

- The strategy and product/service offerings of the organisation: how resilient are they to changing market demands, regulation or customer preference?
- Relationships with partners and competitors: are you part of an open marketplace (such as the Apple App Store), or more of a proprietary, closed operation? How deep is your competitive "moat"? How easy is it to be disintermediated by others?
- From where do you source your goods/services? Are you over-reliant on a single provider for anything? How reliable are they? Can you diversify?
- Your office space: how easily did your staff switch to remote working? How can you make working arrangements more fluid?

- People: how easy is it to hire people with the skills you need? Is the organisation able to attract the right talent? Is it drawing from a sufficiently diverse population? Can you train people in the skills you need? How deep is the skill base – could you survive the loss of a "star" in the organisation? How is the collective mental health and resilience of the organisation?
- Empowerment: to what extent do staff have the knowledge and trust to act for the good of the organisation, without asking for permission and sending questions up the chain of command? A command-and-control structure is good for some situations, but it is inflexible and not always fast.

As you can see, the above questions are more challenging and nuanced, and not always easily answered or solved. What's important is the organisation remains alert and agile, constantly looking outward and tweaking itself to be best placed to respond to whatever the world throws at us next.

## Agree on reporting protocols for risk events

Finally, you should agree with the board what the reporting and escalation protocols around risk events should be. For example, you may wish to offer a deep-dive analysis of all major risk events but only summary reporting around the smaller ones. When do the board need to be informed or consulted, and to what extent do they expect the executive function of the organisation to shoulder the responsibility?

## Summary

Now you have helped your organisation identify the key risks to the achievement of its goals and set the risk appetite for these. You've also set out a process to deal with these risks when they occur and to prevent future occurrences. It's time to look at the key risks in more detail.

# Chapter 6

*Strategic risk*

In Chapter 3, we covered how strategy underpins the entire risk framework of the organisation. Here we cover strategic risk, which is the most important risk for any organisation and sits at the top of our pyramid of risks. This is because, if the organisational strategy is wrong, suboptimal or poorly executed, the organisation will likely not survive. In this case, all other risks cease to matter. To better understand the importance of this risk, in this chapter I'll go into more detail by outlining what it is, how to identify it and how to mitigate against it.

## Understanding strategic risk

Deloitte[48] defines strategic risks as "risks that affect or are created by an organization's business strategy and strategic objectives".[49] BusinessDictionary defines[50] it as follows: "A *possible source of loss that might arise from the pursuit of an unsuccessful business plan. For example, strategic risk might arise from making poor business decisions, from the substandard execution of decisions, from inadequate resource allocation, or from a failure to respond well to changes in the business environment."* Not surprising then that this risk is usually owned by the CEO.

Strategic risk can be explained very simply in practical terms. Actions that an organisation takes (or does not take) lead to risks; think about the risks of entering a new market, launching a new product line, acquiring or divesting a business or choosing a different channel or price point. The right strategic decisions (and actions) lead to exploitation of upside risks – opportunities – which can be the catapult to success. On the other hand, failure to shore up weaknesses can rapidly lead to decline.

Strategic risk is special; it's different in nature to the other risks that a CRO deals with. For example, in *Harvard Business Review*, Robert S. Kaplan and Anette Mikes draw a distinction, arguing that strategic risks are *"different from preventable risks because they are not inherently undesirable"*.[51] Indeed, where a high reward is possible, taking a high strategic risk may be a smart play. They argue that strategic risks require different treatment – it's not about eradicating the risk, it's about adopting *"a risk-management system designed to reduce the probability that the assumed risks actually materialize and to improve the company's ability to manage or contain the risk events should they occur"*.[52] This enables, rather than prevents, the organisation from proceeding with its high-risk and, potentially, high-reward venture, and provides a source of competitive advantage.

Strategic risk is a major consideration for organisations. According to a survey by Deloitte, 81% of companies they asked now explicitly manage strategic risk, rather than limiting their concern to traditional risk areas such as operational, financial and compliance risk.[53]

It seems strategic risk will only grow in importance. The rapidly changing external environment – including the pandemic, distrust in the news, the changing social agenda and further digitisation – is making strategic risk a much more fast-moving and perilous area. Rapid entry by new, innovative disruptors can render incumbent players redundant in blistering timescales. Organisations must be faster than ever to detect early warning signs and respond.

As with all risks, but especially with strategic risk, early detection is key. It might be a slight waning in customer enthusiasm, a drop in a Trustpilot score or some creeping dissatisfaction with customer service. These can quickly escalate from being merely a warning sign to having a traumatic impact on your brand and reputation. Where dissatisfaction and outrage can be communicated and amplified in seconds via a tweet, response times need to be lightning fast. Witness how quickly Amazon deals with a faulty order or how fast Starling Bank is to highlight a great customer review. Look at how perceptions of Facebook changed after the 2016 US election – the exploitation of user data by Cambridge Analytica changed the perception that many have of the platform, perhaps forever. As consumers, how quickly do we decide that a brand is "no longer for us"; that it no longer chimes with our values or our "look"? They of course re-branded to Meta post this event and signal a new future.

The ultimate outcome of a failure of strategic risk management is irrelevance or business oblivion. Below are some examples of strategic risk (and opportunity) in action. Consider these questions and how organisational strategy and risk interacted to create these outcomes:

- What made Xtra-vision fail and Netflix succeed when both organisations initially did the same thing?
- What made Apple phones win and Nokia disappear? (And, also, why do people still love Nokias?)
- Why are customers choosing Starling Bank, N26 and Monzo over incumbent banks?
- Why was the Pixar IPO such a success, and why did Disney acquire them?

- Why did CDs and online music never manage to kill off vinyl?
- Why did video not kill the radio star?

## Assessing your organisation's strategy

This is not a book about how to write a successful strategy for your organisation. That is not the primary role of the CRO. However, as CRO, it's important to remember that the ultimate risk to an organisation's viability is that it pursues the wrong strategy, and so you need to be able to identify problems from the outset.

Poor strategic design is an insidious risk. It's not always immediately apparent when the strategy is wrong. An organisation can be working full tilt and busy making apparent progress, but the expected growth and take-up may just not materialise. It's dispiriting. Often, by the time the issue is recognisable, it can be too late. Indicators of strategic failure are more often "lag" than "lead" indicators, meaning that they only tell you that something is wrong after the fact rather than ahead of time. They can include:

- eroding or stagnant market share;
- failure to expand your foothold with existing customers;
- faltering usage numbers;
- weak customer advocacy; and
- poor performance relative to competitors.

In *The Strategy Book*, Max McKeown defines six measures of success when looking at the design of a strategy. For me, these all speak clearly to the linkage with risk and provide a useful crib sheet when assessing your organisation's strategic design:

- You have thought about different ways your strategy might fail;
- You have considered how leadership styles cope with strategy

problems;

- There is a shared list of things that may go wrong (i.e. risks!);
- You have prepared for what can go wrong in the future (i.e. a risk management plan);
- You have an organisation ready to adapt to future problems; and
- Your strategy is adapted (where possible) to avoid problems.[54]

The best way of insuring against strategic risk is, not surprisingly, for management to invest time and effort in creating the optimal strategy. Once that is done, it should be clearly expressed so employees can easily understand it, with measurable goals and milestones, and it should translate into actionable tactics through the organisation.

In *Good Strategy/Bad Strategy*, Richard P. Rumelt dissects what is wrong with so many corporate strategies today. He reminds us that "*simply being ambitious is not a strategy*" and that "*a good strategy does more than urge us forward towards a goal or vision. A good strategy honestly acknowledges the challenges being faced and provides an approach to overcoming them*".[55] A strategy must be realistic, outward-facing, grounded in the facts. It must be agile; able to flex as the external environment changes. It must be "discriminating", by which I mean it must be precise enough to exclude certain activities – a strategy that is all things to all people is not a strategy at all.

## Areas of strategic risk to consider

The following are particularly topical areas to consider when assessing the effectiveness of your organisation's strategy. These have the potential to either enhance your brand or erode its reputation and value. In many cases, there are rules and regulations which cover some of these areas which will prevent the organisation from making catastrophic mistakes. However, a truly progressive organisation will look beyond the rule of law and overlay their own values to enhance their standing amongst customers.

- **Climate and sustainability**. What is the organisation's sustainability strategy? Are you working towards net zero? From where do you source your products / raw materials? Is your supply chain clean? Can you account for where your goods have passed through?
- **Social responsibility.** Do you use zero-hours contracts? What stability do you offer to your workforce? What rights do they have around notice, holidays and sick pay? Is there an imbalance of power? Is there a union? Would you support one? What is your stance on diversity, equity and inclusion?
- **Tax**. Where does the organisation book its profits? How much tax does it pay? Is there a fair amount of tax being paid in the countries in which you consume the most resources and enjoy their benefits?
- **Customer data**. Where is it stored? What is it used for? Do you share it? Do you use it the way in which customers would want you to? Are you explicit about it? Do you erase it when you no longer need it?
- **Mission**. Finally, and most importantly, what is the organisation's core mission? We can't all be like Patagonia, nicknamed "the coolest company in the world" by some. Their mission statement says it all: "*We're in business to save the planet.*" However, can you say that your organisation is doing something good, at its core, that you and your people can be proud of?

# Exploiting strategic opportunity

At this point, it's worth a reminder that risks can take place which are positive too, often called "upside risks". An upside risk really just identifies what could go better than expected rather than what can go wrong (a downside risk). This is when, for instance, a new product may outperform in a particular market, or find a following in an unexpected geography. A well-designed risk framework can help identify those upside risks too and frame decision-making in order to guide management on their actions. According to Paul Hopkin, it should help a business to figure out whether it should:

- exploit the opportunity so that it definitely happens – taking a step into a new product, market or channel, for example;
- enhance the opportunity, to increase the likelihood of it materialising, e.g. devoting funds to a pilot study or minimum viable product to try out;
- ignore the opportunity – decide that, although it's an interesting opportunity, the company resources are better used elsewhere; or
- share or transfer the opportunity – engage in a joint venture, sell the IP or partner with someone who is better placed to exploit the idea.[56]

# Executing the organisational strategy

Let's assume that the organisational strategy is a good one. You have thoroughly assessed it for strategic risk factors and you believe that it can achieve its aims with the available resources. As we discussed in Chapter 4, a strategy is worthless unless it is fully embedded in the organisation and put into practice every day. However, what's important to note in this context is the factors that contribute towards (or against) the strategy being successfully executed. For example:

- Is the strategy clear? Does it crisply define the USP of the organisation and how it's going to win? Are responsibilities clearly assigned?
- Are there the right number of priorities? If there are too many, there are no priorities at all.
- Have appropriate measures been put in place to determine success?
- Do these measures link to day-to-day goals and milestones?
- Can staff draw a line between what they are doing day-to-day and the overall strategy?
- Is the strategy regularly and consistently reinforced by the entire team? Is it "lived" day-to-day?
- Is the strategy motivating? Does it speak to a mission that your people can get behind? Is it doing some good in the world?

If any of the above factors are missing, it can lead to a disconnect between the strategy as expressed and what staff are actually doing day-to-day. This is a dangerous risk because it is not immediately apparent that something is wrong. Strategy design may be fine and everything can look great on paper, but somehow, each quarter, it's not yielding the results it should. Staff are becoming demotivated, stressed or overworked. Management and the board are frustrated and wondering why people "just don't get it". When this happens, it pays to look at whether there's a problem with strategy execution.

## Summary

As a new or aspiring CRO, start by looking at strategic risk, both its design and its execution. Assuming the organisation has designed an excellent strategy, with a clear vision and measurable goals, and has set the organisation up in pursuit of those goals, it now needs a motivated, aligned and talented team to execute it. This brings us on to people risk.

# Chapter 7

*People risk*

Once you are comfortable with the design and execution of the organisational strategy, you need the people to execute it. An organisation is only as good as the people it can attract and retain. The head of HR or Chief People Officer (CPO) is the obvious owner of people-related risks. That said, culture comes from the top, from the CEO and leadership team, and of course, every employee has the ability to create risk through their own conduct.

## Understanding people risk

The Institute of Operational Risk defines people risk as *"the risk that people do not follow the organization's procedures, practices and/or rules, thus deviating from expected behaviour in a way that could damage the business's performance and reputation"*.[57] It equates people risk with conduct risk, explained below, which I think is too narrow a definition.

I personally take a much broader view of risks relating to people, incorporating the areas of diversity, conduct, culture, incentives, productivity, health and wellness, employee data privacy and reputation. Another angle to people risk is the risk of not being able to attract, hire or retain the right people for your organisation at the right cost.

Let's look at an example. If social media is to be believed, there appears to be something of a cultural crisis taking place in the computer gaming industry. As a sector dominated by young, bright individuals, you would expect it to be espousing some of the better work practices and employee experiences. However, as the race to the market accelerates and games (and user expectations) grow in size and ambition, it has led in some cases to pressure on staff to work at a level that is unsustainable. So-called "crunch" culture is getting a lot of attention at the moment, and it can be seen as a source of people risk. Those companies overworking their employees will eventually severely impact the wellbeing of their staff, leading to an unhealthy culture and potentially loss of talent, inability to hire and reputational damage. The thinking is that nobody minds the occasional, temporary situation when they have to work extremely hard in order to get a delivery over the line. However, the expectation is that once that delivery is achieved, there is a period when workload eases off, staff can take back some of that time in lieu, repay the attention debts to their families and loved ones and "reset" before the next wave comes. However, when that crunch period extends beyond a few weeks into months or even years, it becomes toxic and unmanageable.

## Understanding conduct risk

Conduct risk is a relatively new area of risk that was borne out of financial market misconduct issues such as LIBOR-fixing and PPI mis-selling. These were reputational crises in financial services, where banks were found to be acting in ways that breached customer trust.

KPMG defines conduct risk as "*any action of a financial institution or individual that leads to customer detriment, or has an adverse effect on market stability or effective competition*".[58] There are varying definitions, but the concepts of actions taken by people leading to customer detriment are the essence of conduct risk, and that is why I have included it within people risk.

## Measuring the potential for people risk

It's important to begin by assessing people risk in your organisation to ensure that any problems bubbling under the surface are dealt with quickly and before any incidents occur. Measures which can be used to gauge the health of people risk include the following:

- Employee engagement scores e.g. using anonymous survey platforms such as Officevibe;
- Glassdoor reviews;
- Absenteeism;
- Number of unfilled vacancies;
- Productivity measures;
- Staff turnover percentage. Despite a common perception that employee turnover should be as low as possible, demonstrating loyalty and workplace happiness, there can be cases where turnover is too low. New employees bring fresh perspectives, new ideas and ways of working. A culture that never changes can become stagnant; and
- Qualitative and quantitative feedback from exit interviews.

Tools for measuring the potential for conduct risk include:

- Product satisfaction scores;
- Net Promoter Score (the willingness of customers to recommend a product or company);
- Customer complaints (a lag indicator); and

- In financial services, signs of customer financial distress (where customers are unable to service their loans).

## Developing a people risk framework

Managing people risk requires a multi-faceted approach. These approaches are almost all focused on starting early and embedding thoughtful strategy into hiring and training practices as well as staff care into day-to-day operations. As you might expect, the CPO and human resources will be responsible for most of these activities, but the CRO has responsibility to ensure that they have taken a broad enough view and are following through on their action plan. Important elements of the people risk management strategy should include:

- **Strategic resource and talent planning**. Efficient HR management starts with the organisation's strategy. Staff need to understand what it's trying to achieve and the specific talent requirements needed to deliver it. This will prevent suboptimal hiring decisions and ensure the organisation is resourced to deliver. A motivating, successful, sustainable strategy that's seen to be working is the ultimate recruitment tool.
- **Succession planning.** Succession planning serves as the gap analysis for your bench in the organisation. It forces management to think about their critical people, their upcoming talent and what needs to be done to address gaps and minimise key person risk.
- **A well-defined recruitment strategy**. This will create a healthy pipeline of talent and should include supporting the organisation with position management, advertising, screening, interviewing, selecting and onboarding new staff.
- **A motivating onboarding and induction journey**. This should include overseeing a new recruit's all-important first

contact with the organisation and speeding the transition of new staff into value contributors.

- **Encouraging staff engagement.** Healthy organisations deliberately assess the level of staff engagement in the organisation and foster open dialogue with staff to ensure they feel bought in and that any problems are caught early on and resolved.
- **Clear performance management processes.** Clear goals, policies and processes for assessment of staff performance, values and behaviours should be set. Human resources should be supporting management through these processes and linking them to promotion, development and remuneration.
- **Staff development and talent management.** This should take into account the needs of the organisation, creating a framework for how staff will learn and develop, both on the job and in formal training sessions. This should include the identification of high-potential individuals and the management of their journey through the organisation.
- **Fair reward frameworks.** Setting a clear and motivating reward framework for the organisation in collaboration with the board of directors or a separate remuneration committee. This includes everything from executive pay to overall pay ranges, role descriptions and promotion criteria. It should embrace fixed and variable compensation and a wider set of employee benefits beyond money – the value proposition of each role. For example, this could mean training and development opportunities, flexible working and a great office environment.
- **Management of appealing employee benefits.** Offering a suite of lifestyle benefits that will attract and retain the people the organisation wants. This might include remote working support, health insurance, gym membership or season ticket loans.

- **Support for smooth termination, resignation and redundancy processes.** Supporting the different ways in which staff can exit an organisation is critical. Managing these processes fairly and equitably minimises legal risk and hopefully ensures the employees leave with a positive view of the organisation and continue to act as advocates.
- **Professional legal advice and handling of employee-employer relations.** Human resources and legal should advise management in understanding, interpreting and applying employment law and regulation fairly, equitably and consistently in all dealings with staff. This might include:
- **Grievances.** Managing the process where an employee is dissatisfied with some aspect of their treatment and has made a complaint.
- **Disciplinary and capability processes.** Supporting management in dealing with issues of underperformance of staff members.

It should be noted that the above measures, such as fair reward and attractive benefits, are only the beginning of what an organisation and its CPO will want to put in place – these days, with the war for talent very much in favour of the employee, your people team will be striving for a work environment that supports self-actualisation, inclusion and equity and motivating career opportunities in order to attract the best talent.

## Developing a conduct risk framework

The greatest weapons an organisation has to counter conduct risk are a good underlying culture and a strong set of values. The board, CEO, CRO and leadership team must set out clearly the expectations of behaviour in the organisation. The right culture will naturally provoke understanding of and empathy with your customer (i.e. "would you sell this product to your friend?") and should prevent many risks occurring in the first place. Other steps include clear product guidelines, ethics policies, new product sign-off processes and customer feedback loops. However, without an underlying set of values, these are just the icing without the cake.

In addition, the measures below should enable early warning of problems, ensuring risks can be quickly controlled.

- **An ethical business structure.** By segregating duties to avoid conflicts of interest, the very structure of the organisation is a mitigant against conduct risk. Ensure there is a balance of voices as the organisation assesses strategic and product options.
- **Adequate supervision**. Having adequate oversight, both qualitative and quantitative, of staff and their dealings with customers will ensure any training needs are picked up quickly when someone starts to stray outside of the guidelines. For example, a call centre supervisor listening to a sample of customer calls on a regular basis.
- **Complaints monitoring**. Keeping a sharp eye on trends from customer complaints and feedback can provide an indication if something is amiss in terms of employee conduct.
- **In-house whistleblowing mechanism.** Offering a mechanism for employees to "blow the whistle" on wrongdoing will allow problems to be picked up more quickly than if there is a culture of silencing those who highlight problems. This area may be overseen by the risk or compliance department, or an independent third party.
- **Personal account dealing and transaction monitoring.** Where the company trades in financial instruments, and where employees may have access to material non-public information, it's necessary to oversee, and sometimes prohibit, the trades that employees themselves undertake.

- **Communications monitoring.** This involves looking at both structured outbound communications and ad hoc responses to customer queries to ensure they are appropriate.
- **Information barriers.** Where conflicts of interest exist within an organisation, having a firewall in place to ensure inappropriate information does not cross company lines is critical.

## Emerging people risks and opportunities

In the aftermath of Covid-19 and the resultant single biggest change to our working habits in living memory, there are a new set of considerations for organisations to work with. The advent of home working has necessitated a long overdue pivot to a more trust-based method of people management, focused on achieving objectives rather than hours in the office. Employee onboarding, mentoring, training and development need to be reconsidered in this new world of fluid, virtual working. With some employees making a permanent shift to remote working, away from cities and even to different countries, the value proposition for roles needs to change. Workers feel that being able to work from home two to three days per week is as valuable as a pay rise of up to 8%.[59] Progressive organisations will be reviewing this new modality as a way to attract and incentivise the best people. However, those that don't move with the times and offer flexible working could lose their talent and struggle to hire the skills they need in order to function and grow in the future.

### Summary

Your people are your greatest asset. If people risk is managed well, you have a key strategic advantage over your competitors. Mismanaged people risk can lead to public and messy consequences and can be a huge distraction. We now move on to another source of competitive advantage or disadvantage – your technology.

# Chapter 8

*Technology risk*

Technology is now so core to the workings of organisations that it is a high priority when considering risk management. It sometimes *is* the source of the strategy: the competitive advantage. From pizza delivery to taxi companies, from new entrants in online banking to social media, technology opportunities – and the associated risks – are huge and require a sophisticated and evolving set of controls to manage them.

Technology and digital risks are the primary responsibility of the Chief Technology Officer (CTO). However, in truth, some areas such as data privacy go far beyond technology; data privacy requires end-to-end consideration and governance through the life cycle of data management. However, given that responsibility for data storage often rests with the technology teams, I have included it here.

## Understanding technology risk

Technology risk is the risk of any failure in the end-to-end technology platform disrupting the organisation's functioning. It could include any compromise in the confidentiality, integrity and availability of information.

The move to the cloud has been a global good, slashing infrastructure housing costs and building greater agility, resilience and redundancy into IT architecture. It outsources a whole area of IT platform management, or rather it replaces it with another set of skills required to manage and oversee virtual environments. When Covid hit, those organisations whose technology resided in the cloud found the migration to remote working to be smooth and, in many cases, seamless. Those on outdated, on-premise technology had to move quickly to react. However, this pivot to cloud technology has also resulted in heavy reliance on a small number of providers: Amazon AWS, Microsoft Azure and a few others. This consolidation brings other risks, such as concentration risk relating to platforms. Plus, there are still issues such as data privacy, regional data strategies and General Data Protection Regulation (GDPR) and other privacy legislation to content with. So, we have evolved, but we have also traded one set of challenges for another. Our day-to-day working has become so reliant on these technology behemoths that we need to be thinking about them as critical utilities, in the same way we think of power, water and food chain providers.

There are two further subsets within technology risk: cybersecurity risk and data privacy risk.

Cybersecurity risk is specifically the risk of loss or damage to the organisation's information systems. It's usually associated with events such as cyberattacks, ransomware and denial of service attacks.

Data privacy risk is the risk that data is compromised or not used in accordance with its intended purpose. Under GDPR in the EU, organisations that fail to uphold data privacy standards are liable to fines of up to 4% of their annual turnover, not to mention significant reputational risk.

## Information security standards

Although it was developed in the '90s, it is still relevant to think about technology risks using the CIA model: confidentiality, integrity and availability. Your systems must be kept secure, they must be trusted to be accurate and they must be available and online as needed. Two information security frameworks that can help you to assess the technology risks within your organisation are ISO27001 and COBIT 5.

The most prevalent Information security framework is ISO27001, which proposes 14 categories of information security protection. This can be used as a starting point to assess the information security status of an organisation. They are:

1) Information Security Policies;
2) Organisation of Information Security;
3) Human Resource Security;
4) Asset Management;
5) Access Control;
6) Cryptography;
7) Physical and Environmental Security;
8) Operations Security;
9) Communications Security;
10) System Acquisition and Maintenance;
11) Supplier Relationships;
12) Security Incident Management;
13) Business Continuity Management; and
14) Compliance.[60]

In addition, COBIT 5 (Control Objectives for Information and Related Technologies), developed by ISACA (Information

Systems Audit and Control Association), is a useful model of governance and management objectives for information security. As well as the core reference model, it allows you to tailor the model to your organisation's circumstances. COBIT has five key principles:

1. Meeting stakeholder needs;
2. Covering the enterprise end-to-end;
3. Applying a single, integrated framework;
4. Enabling a holistic approach; and
5. Separating governance from management.[61]

It also has five component parts:

1. A framework of governance objectives and good practices by IT domain;
2. Process descriptions which map to the four areas of plan, build, run and monitor;
3. Control objectives for effective control of each IT process;
4. Management guidelines; and
5. Maturity models, which allow you to look at how developed your IT platform is.[62]

Whether you choose to get certified in these models or not, the frameworks above provide a useful starting point for discussion with the CTO about the maturity of the technology function.

## Cybersecurity

The increasing interconnectedness of our digital world shows no sign of abating. We continue to produce and share more data exponentially, and we create new ways of integrating digital convenience into our lives. The advent of big data, cloud computing, APIs and numerous other developments bring a world of possibilities to individuals and organisations, but they also open us up to cyberattacks that seek to exploit these networks and technologies. To protect our systems and stay safe, organisations need a strong cybersecurity framework.

## Developing a cybersecurity framework

An effective strategy will typically incorporate the following elements:

*Understanding of business context*

- **Business goals**. As with all risk areas, it's important to begin with what the organisation is looking to achieve. For example, how many customers will it have? In how many markets does it anticipate trading?
- **Risk management strategy**. Once the business goals are understood, your cyber team can outline a proportionate risk management strategy; one that grows as the business does.
- **Culture, awareness and training**. Staff need to be informed of the risk management strategy, remain risk-aware and be kept up to date on current threats. As the ongoing success of phishing attacks shows, social engineering is still often the easiest way to infiltrate an organisation.

*Anticipation of threats*

- **Cyber intelligence**. A programme should be put in place to regularly scour for new threats to the organisation's perimeter and data, from both internal and external expert sources.
- **Regular testing**. Regular penetration testing and vulnerability scanning of the technology platform should take place, as well as remediation of the weaknesses found. Red team testing is a particular type of concentrated penetration testing. Phishing testing checks the awareness of your people to a range of attacks.
- **Resilience and recovery protocols**. Measures should be put in place to ensure that the organisation can withstand, respond to and recover from cyberattacks.

*Protection of assets*

- **Asset identification and management**. This is about knowing what assets you are trying to protect, what the entry points to the organisation are and maintaining an up-to-date inventory.
- **Policies and procedures**. These should govern roles and responsibilities, response protocols and escalation. They should also cover information about trusted third parties who can provide support.
- **Access control**. Policies should maintain "least privilege" access to critical resources, and ensure that all access is logged and attributable.
- **Data security**. The use of encryption and layering of security controls, especially over sensitive functions such as payments.
- **Tools and preventive maintenance.** A suite of up-to-date tools and protections should be maintained.

*Detection of threats*

- **24-7 monitoring across all critical assets**. There should be round-the-clock monitoring and surveillance in place, with notification of any security breaches and a process for following up.
- **Exception reporting and escalation**. There should be a protocol for on-call staff to be notified, including out of hours, for initial triage of the incident and for appropriate escalation, depending on its severity.

*Response protocols*

- **Notification and escalation protocols**. Per the above, this includes bringing the right people together, including third-party experts, to analyse the incident and propose the way forward.

- **Analysis process**. A clear process should be developed that allows for quick and consistent investigation of the threat to prompt action and learning. For example, how severe is the threat? Where has it come from? What systems and data have been impacted? Is it still underway?
- **Containment and eradication**. These should include processes to isolate the affected area of technology, neutralise the risk and restore normal operations.
- **Communications**. There should be clear methods to notify and mobilise the key staff, plus notification of all staff if, for example, systems are compromised.
- **Learning and improvement**. Having a post-mortem process, understanding what went wrong and strengthening systems so the same event cannot happen again is essential to improving cybersecurity.

*Software vendor risk*

Finally, organisations must bear in mind the need for full, end-to-end technology platform risk management. In our highly-connected digital world, organisations often have dozens of software suppliers on which they rely, and therefore the risks are not only in-house. It's imperative to examine the software supply chain and to work in partnership with suppliers, customers and other stakeholders in order to build true security resilience. Recent issues such as the malicious Sunburst attack on Solarwinds and the Log4Shell vulnerability only serve to remind us of the threats that exist.

## The NIST Cybersecurity Framework

The US Department of Commerce's National Institute of Standards and Technology (NIST) developed the NIST Cybersecurity Framework to help organisations of all sizes to assess and address their cyber risks.[63] It's free of charge and downloadable from their website.

The framework consists of three elements:

1) The framework's "core" is a set of cybersecurity activities that mirror some of the components of risk management that I outlined above. They include five "functions" as they relate to cyber risks: Identify; Protect; Defend; Respond; and Recover.

2) It then has a set of four "tiers" of competence: Tier 1 – Partial; Tier 2 – Risk-informed; Tier 3 – Repeatable; and Tier 4 – Adaptive.

3) Finally, a framework *"profile represents the outcomes based on business needs"*.[64]

The detailed controls in the framework range from key management, to access control, to response planning, communications and detection and analysis. While a voluntary framework, it is widely used as a useful standard to assess your cybersecurity framework and to provide a common language and objective assessment. When reviewed by a cyber team with the requisite skill set, it allows you to quickly identify where your areas for improvement might be, and where to prioritise investment. For example, you may be at level 3 when it comes to access control, but only level 1 in detecting external threats – this provides you with the beginnings of a plan to address your weaknesses.

## Data privacy

Data privacy took on a whole new level of significance with the introduction of the General Data Protection Regulation, or GDPR. Originally launched by the EU in 2016, it was brought into UK law via the UK Data Protection Act of 2018. GDPR and data privacy issues are overseen in the UK by the Information Commissioner's Office, or ICO. At time of writing, the Data

Reform Bill in the UK is being debated; it aims to reduce the burden of some aspects of GDPR compliance and may impact the provisions below.

GDPR[65] applies to the processing of personal data. It defines certain roles pertaining to data processing, including data processor and data controller, and requires you to be clear what your role is in each case. It specifies certain data pertaining to the customer as "personal", and it affords customers eight rights regarding their data:

- The right to information (i.e. to know what data is held about them);
- The right of access (i.e. to be able to get a copy of that data);
- The right to rectification (e.g. if there is an inaccuracy in their data);
- The right to erasure (sometimes called the right to "be forgotten");
- The right to restriction of processing (i.e. to say you don't want to have your data processed in a certain way);
- The right to data portability (e.g. from one provider to another);
- The right to object to the use of their data; and
- The right to avoid automated decision-making (i.e. not to have a decision made solely by a computer model).

It affords customers the right to make a Data Subject Access Request (DSAR), to see what data an organisation holds on them and how it's being used.

GDPR introduces a duty for public authorities or bodies, or those who carry out certain types of processing activities, to appoint a Data Protection Officer (DPO). DPOs help to monitor internal compliance, inform and advise on data protection obligations, provide advice regarding Data Protection Impact Assessments (DPIAs) and act as a contact point for data subjects and the ICO.

The DPO must be independent, an expert in data protection and adequately resourced, and they must report to the highest management level. A DPO can be an existing employee or externally appointed and, in some cases, several organisations can appoint a single DPO between them to minimise costs.

GDPR also requires organisations to perform a DPIA[66] when you make a change to how you're processing data that could affect the end customer.

The GDPR stipulates that organisations must ensure that all personal data collected and processed is:

- collected in a fair, lawful and transparent manner;
- accurate and kept up to date;
- collected for a specified, explicit and legitimate purpose;
- adequate, relevant and processed only where it is necessary for the purposes for which it is collected;
- retained for the minimum period required for its purpose; and
- safeguarded by comprehensive and proportionate governance measures.

Bear in mind that, while people mostly think about customer data when considering data privacy, employee and other stakeholder data is subject to the same protections e.g. employee addresses, national insurance numbers, payroll information, etc.

## Developing a data privacy framework

When developing a data privacy framework, you should include the following control elements:

- A data privacy policy, including an awareness of which data regimes the organisation is subject to (e.g. EU, US, Singapore, Switzerland etc.);
- Assignment of a DPO (the person responsible for data privacy);
- Inventory of data assets;
- Securing and segregation of data assets;
- Access controls over key data updates (ideally, this should be updated by system processes and not people, who are inherently less reliable);
- Logging of changes to key data, audit trails and backups;
- Regular cyber vulnerability checks and maintenance;
- Staff training and awareness; and
- DSAR process i.e. how to respond when someone asks your organisation to uncover what data you hold on them.

## Summary

The growth in technology opportunities – and risks – continues unabated. The technology landscape requires a significant amount of the CRO's attention. Proactive management of cyber, data and privacy risks, combined with a clear technology architecture and plan, will set the organisation up for success. Now that the fundamental areas of strategy, people and technology risk have been considered, it's time to turn to the financial risks facing the organisation.

# Chapter 9

## *Financial risk*

We are dealing with a dramatically changed economic landscape; the combination of a pandemic, conflict and economic headwinds makes for a complex and challenging environment for CROs. Covid did not impact all areas in the same way. Big tech companies got even bigger whereas parts of the high street got wiped out, with many small businesses on life support. There is a heavy hangover of Covid bounce-back loans to be repaid. Looking to the future, Government fiscal strategy will have to figure out how to pay for the massive debts incurred. At the time of writing, interest rates are creeping up from historically low levels and debt levels are enormous. Crypto currency has suffered huge drops and a loss of confidence. There's a potential big hangover coming to the buy now pay later sector. This is all to say that the financial risk for many organisations is at an all-time high.

Financial risks are among some of the best understood and most easily quantifiable risks. They are, of course, devastating if not properly managed. It is largely the responsibility of the Chief Financial Officer (CFO) to understand, oversee and mitigate the financial risks facing the organisation. However, credit risk may be the responsibility of the Chief Credit Officer or CRO. In this chapter, we deconstruct financial risk and look at how to manage it.

## Understanding financial risk

Financial risk can be broken down into a number of sub-risks, including:

Capital and liquidity

- **Capital or solvency risk.** The risk of not having enough capital to run your business. In today's startup culture, having a reliable source of capital and a "runway" to your next capital injection is key.
- **Liquidity risk.** The risk of not having enough cash to meet your debts as they fall due.
- Credit and counterparty
- **Credit risk.** The risk of someone, usually a customer, not paying you as expected. On a macro level, it is the risk of your credit portfolio not operating in line with your expectations.
- **Counterparty risk.** The probability that one of those involved in a transaction might default on their contractual obligation. Counterparty risk is particularly relevant for organisations that take part in credit, investment and trading transactions.

Market

- **Market risk.** The risk of experiencing losses or gains due to the financial markets moving adversely/positively for you.

Financial reporting

- **Financial reporting risk.** The risk of the organisation failing to produce timely and accurate financial statements.

## Developing a capital and liquidity risk framework

These are basic tenets of good capital and liquidity management that should be embedded in the financial risk framework.

- If in startup mode, the organisation should have a clear understanding of how many months or years of operating costs it has available with existing capital levels and allow sufficient time for capital raising, including some contingency.
- Capital injections should be tied to performance milestones within the organisation and tracked with rigour and learning, evidencing that each capital injection is resulting in a more valuable business.
- Liquidity metrics and cash flow levels should be regularly monitored. Remember that a period of rapid growth in an organisation can be one of the most perilous times from a liquidity perspective, as working capital requirements grow.
- The finance team should have a solid understanding of the pattern of spend throughout the financial year and the working capital requirements to accommodate this.

Liquidity refers to the ability to meet short-term debts as they fall due. Solvency refers to the long-term viability of the organisation. Both are important for the organisation to manage well. If a company cannot meet its short-term debts, it will rapidly run into severe problems. However, if its capital structure is not right, if it's too overloaded with debt, this is also not a viable situation. Some commonly used measures to gauge liquidity and solvency are shown below:

**Liquidity ratios:**

Current ratio = Current assets / Current liabilities

Liquid or "quick" ratio = (Current assets minus stock) / Current liabilities

**Solvency ratios:**

Debt to Assets = Total debt / Total assets

Debt to Equity = Total debt / Total equity

Times interest earned = Earnings before interest, tax, depreciation and amortisation or "EBITDA" / Interest expense

As CRO, you want to see that your CFO and finance function have a well-formed view of the financial future of the organisation, the capital structure and the ability to pay debts. They should be well aware of how much "runway" they have to pay debts and function. They should be aware of cash flows, and the organisation, unless in startup mode, should be cash-flow positive. They should have a system of metrics that will alert them to, for example, whether customers are taking too long to pay, or stock levels are rising, or sales are slowing.

# Developing a credit and counterparty risk framework

Credit risk is a complex area and is itself the subject of a substantial amount of writing. While full in-depth coverage of this topic is beyond the scope of this book, below I include the fundamental concepts of a sound credit risk framework. However, first, it's important to distinguish between institutional and retail credit management.

# Institutional credit

Institutional credit refers to lending to governments, large corporations and municipal bodies. Compared to retail lending, which is more heavily regulated, there are no real constraints on this type of lending, other than that the purposes must be legal. The lending organisation sets its risk appetite for what sectors and industries it wishes to lend to, the seniority and duration of the debt and the limits. It sources the funds for lending, matches up the tenor (short-term vs. long term) of the money being borrowed and the money it lends out, agrees the terms and undertakings or "covenants" the customer makes and monitors the portfolio through its life cycle, perhaps repackaging or divesting the debt along the way.

Subcategories of credit risk in the institutional space are as follows:

- **Default or issuer risk**. The risk the client doesn't repay.
- **Downgrade risk.** The risk that the quality of the debt deteriorates due to an event affecting the borrower; so, for example, if the credit rating of the country or company disimproves, you are left holding debt at a certain risk level and interest rate that may no longer be appropriate.
- **Country risk.** A change to the profile and stability of the country of the borrower.
- **Transaction or settlement risk.** Risk of a failure in the settlement of the loan.
- **Mitigation failure risk.** The risk that the hedging instruments put in place fail to offset the risk of a particular loan or group of loans.
- **Concentration risk.** The risk that too much lending is concentrated in one particular sector or type of client, leading to big losses if a systematic issue arises.

- **Wrong-way risk.** This is when credit exposure to a counterparty is negatively correlated with the credit quality of that counterparty. In other words, the more likely it is for the counterparty to default, the greater the exposure to that counterparty. It also occurs when a downgrade to a borrower also affects the security of the loan.

## Retail lending

Retail lending, in the UK at least, refers to lending to individuals and sole traders, below a certain transaction size. The rules around retail lending are more prescriptive and contain more protections for the borrower, which means there are additional credit and operational risks to a lending organisation.

Retail lending in the UK is subject to Consumer Credit Association regulations and FCA consumer credit sourcebook (CONC) rules. They cover regulated credit agreements, where:

- the credit agreement relates to unsecured credit of up to £25,000; and
- the legal entity of the business applying for credit is a sole trader.

CONC 5.2[67] says: *"A firm must undertake a reasonable assessment of the creditworthiness of a customer before entering into (or increasing) a regulated credit agreement."* This means that, before agreeing to lend to a retail customer, you must ensure the loan is affordable for them, taking into account their current financial situation. This includes understanding their income and expenditure and even their cost of living. The customer is usually allowed a cooling-off period for two weeks after a loan if they change their mind. CONC also prescribes certain documentation that must be sent to the customer e.g. if the interest rate changes or the customer fails to make a payment.

Given how rigorous these legal requirements are, there should be key controls embedded to ensure that these are actioned:

- The organisation should have a clear policy that outlines the types of customers they lend to and the steps taken to ensure they are creditworthy.
- There should be a process to get a clear understanding of the source of funds, including validating the customer's income and how they will repay the loan.
- There should be clear and consistent policy rules that outline which customers the organisation will accept and which they will exclude. They should be applied fairly and consistently.
- Clear records should be kept of the data used at the time of the decision and of any judgements that were applied.

## Overall credit risk management

The Bank for International Settlements[68] defined 17 "Principles for the Management of Credit Risk", which are long-standing and useful. Here, I distil these into three overall areas.

- The organisation should have a sound credit risk framework.
- The organisation should manage credit appropriately through the entire loan life cycle.
- The organisation should monitor credit risk and take remedial action when required.

## Credit risk framework

As CRO, you should be looking for the following to be in place in your credit organisation.

- Credit policy. An overall credit policy that outlines the type of lending the organisation does, its eligibility criteria, its process for setting and reviewing lending limits and its

approach when borrowers fail to pay.
- Roles and responsibilities for credit management, including who can sign off loans to what level of exposure.
- Segregation of duties between those who initiate the credit and make money from it (the "front office" or first line) and those who provide independent oversight (the credit team, or second line). The incentives of the credit team should not be linked to overall revenue performance.
- Well-staffed credit teams who are adequately skilled, trained, listened to and motivated.
- Supervision and governance, including from adequately skilled board members.

## Managing credit through the loan life cycle

*Risks at origination*

A good place to start is to consider how credit assessment decisions are made. A credit policy sets the strategy for the lending organisation and underpins all future lending decisions. Lenders sometimes refer to the "five Cs" of credit to gauge the creditworthiness of potential borrowers. These are as follows:

- **Character**. This is shown by the applicant's credit history and their propensity to pay loans back in the past.
- **Capacity**. This is the applicant's ability to pay, sometimes looked at through ratios such as debt-to-income, or by looking at their income vs. expenditure patterns. Expected revenues from the business, and their reliability, are a key consideration here.
- **Capital.** The financial resources an applicant has and the sources of their capital.
- **Collateral.** If a loan is to be secured, what assets can act as security for the loan? It could be a property or other asset, it could be future revenues, or the loan may be unsecured.

- **Conditions.** The purpose of the loan, the amount involved, the term and the applicable interest rate.[69]

To avoid the risk of being accused of being unfair or favouring/ not favouring certain customers, it's critical that your credit risk policy outlines the criteria for lending, and that these are applied consistently. If the organisation refuses to lend to a customer, it's important to document which assessment criteria they didn't meet, and that these are clear and objective. For large-scale retail lending, organisations are starting to make use of machine learning and financial models to apply their credit criteria. I discuss the use of models for decisioning in Chapter 14.

## Risk during the loan life cycle

Having carefully applied the credit assessment criteria up front, it's important to track the performance of both individual loans and the overall portfolio. Your chief credit officer will have set expectations for how the portfolio will perform, both in terms of revenue and credit losses. Monitoring how these expectations stack up against reality is key to identify issues early. Although your portfolio expectations will inform the projected interest income and delinquency levels of the loan book, these are only predictions. The credit team monitors the true performance of the book against those expectations and should regularly update the financial forecast as a result. Some key metrics in this area include:

- Interest income
- Amount and percentage of loans in arrears (often stratified into 30, 60, 90 days overdue)
- Expected credit losses (the amount and percentage of losses expected, given the risk profile of the portfolio)
- Loss given default (if all the customers in arrears actually default on their loans, what will the losses be?)

One key risk to watch for is concentration risk. Most portfolios come with an expectation of a blend of customer types and industries in order to spread the risk and avoid concentration. This "portfolio effect" should mitigate against major credit losses from individual borrowers. However, where the organisation finds that its exposures are highly concentrated in a smaller number of borrowers, this leaves it more vulnerable to bigger swings in performance. For example, one fintech lender faced huge losses in 2021 because it lent large sums to just 10 borrowers – most of which were property developers. This is a good illustration of concentration risk as well as performance risk due to environmental factors, as Covid had a traumatic effect on many of these companies.

*Risks during collections, recovery and closeout*

A sad but inevitable aspect of lending is that a proportion of customers will have difficulty repaying their loans, either due to short-term financial difficulty (from which they may emerge successfully), or in the longer term, a more serious change in circumstances. This is a situation where the character of an organisation shows through. How it deals with those customers will impact upon the organisation's reputation and its finances.

*Vulnerability*

In the retail lending space, one key risk to watch out for at this point in the lending cycle is

customer vulnerability. The FCA defines a vulnerable person as "someone who, due to their personal circumstances, is especially susceptible to harm, particularly when a firm doesn't act with appropriate levels of care". They outline four drivers of vulnerability:

- low resilience;
- low capability;
- suffering a negative life event; or
- having an ongoing health condition that affects day-to-day activities.[70]

Customers can become vulnerable due to a number of reasons, from illness to mental health to a change in financial circumstances. Your front-line staff need to be trained to detect signs of vulnerability and to tailor their approach accordingly. Vulnerable customers need to be tagged as such in your systems, and you need to evidence the approach taken to define them as vulnerable and to make the appropriate adjustments and concessions. Showing restraint and empathy in this situation, while still observing the legal agreement, is a nuanced challenge.

The FCA conducted research into people classed as vulnerable and identified five practices by lenders that caused particular problems. They were:

- Failure to provide clear explanations;
- Inappropriate and predatory sales behaviours;
- Technological innovation and digital exclusion;
- Poor frontline interaction; and
- Rigid product design and service structures.[71]

To mitigate risks during this phase of the lending cycle, the credit and customer service teams should:

- Ensure operational rigour around customer notifications to ensure they are kept up to date on what is required from them and when. This should ideally include automated notifications and customer self-service using technology, allowing them, when appropriate, to make payments without needing to speak to an agent. Software offerings such as

Webio (www.webio.io) offer solutions in this space.

- Develop a clear and compassionate collections policy.
- Train its people, and then train them again. Develop an awareness and an empathetic mindset towards vulnerability.
- Develop a vulnerability framework that will define and tag those customers who are likely to default on their loans, incorporating training and awareness, a flexible policy and the ability to identify and flag customers.
- Ensure adequate documentation and notification. It sounds obvious, but it's critically important to ensure that customers are notified promptly and properly that they are falling into arrears. They need regular reminders, ideally via multiple channels, and should be offered links to various debt support groups.

Approaching financial distress and vulnerability appropriately is the right thing to do morally. It's also necessary from a risk management perspective, as failure to get these measures right can potentially jeopardise the enforceability of the loan book.

*Collections, recoveries, refinancing and closeout*
At the end of the loan cycle, either the facility gets repaid and closed out, or, in the event of failure to pay, as a lending organisation, you have certain options. Your credit policy should support the following decisions.

- How the organisation treats non-performing loans / debtors (including taking legal action or using a recoveries agency to buy the loan book at a discount and chase down the debt); and
- Whether the organisation takes out credit insurance, either on an individual loan basis or on your portfolio as a whole.

Finally, at the end of the process, there should be clear processes for releasing any security held once the loan is repaid. If you are continuing the customer relationship, your front-line team will be discussing refinancing or rolling over the financing arrangements well in advance of the termination date.

## Counterparty risk

Related to credit risk, counterparty risk is more about a financial counterparty failing in its obligations to you. It could be that you have taken out a hedging instrument or derivative and the counterparty refuses to pay. Or an insurance company failing to pay out on a risk event. Subcategories of risk in this area are:

- Performance risk – the risk the counterparty fails to perform what they were supposed to;
- Replacement risk – the risk that you are unable to find an equivalent product/service to meet your needs;
- Settlement risk – specific to financial services, the risk that an intermediary bank fails to settle the transaction properly.

Controls to mitigate or reduce counterparty risk include careful selection of counterparties up front, diversification of your counterparties to avoid over-reliance and taking out insurance against the risk. This risk is similar to third-party/supplier risk, which I discuss further in Chapter 10.

## Developing a market risk framework

As mentioned, market risk arises when the markets move against (or with) you, affecting your financial position. There are four commonly recognised subcategories of market risk, which relate to the underlying thing that is moving. They are:

- Interest rate risk
- Foreign exchange (FX) risk
- Commodity risk
- Equity risk

So, if you have a loan taken out that is based on the UK bank borrowing rate, and that rate unexpectedly increases, you have experienced interest rate risk. Similarly, if you pay for goods in one currency, but get paid in another, and those currencies shift in relation to each other (and you haven't hedged the position), you experience FX risk, and so on.

While this risk can exist for any organisation that has debt or trades in foreign markets, it is even more pertinent in those organisations which perform investment and trading as their core business. For those specialist organisations, there will need to be a much fuller exposition of the risks and controls than can be provided here.

At a basic level, the following strategies should be used to mitigate against the key market risks.

- As always, responsibility for market risk management should be clearly defined.
- A market risk management policy should detail the organisation's appetite and limits for market risk and its strategy for whether or not to hedge exposures.
- The organisation should have an understanding of and report regularly on its market risk exposures, such as to interest rates and foreign exchange movements.
- Systems should be in place that capture the key positions, movements and trigger points. So, what holdings (e.g. debts, investments, receivables) does the organisation have that are subject to market risk movements, what is

the underlying index that affects their value, and what is the current position, plus expected future movement of those indices?

- Risk appetite should be clearly defined, including points at which escalation is necessary or at which there is a need to stop an activity altogether. So, the organisation may be willing to tolerate a certain amount of foreign exchange losses, but may wish to hedge its exposure above a certain amount. Hedging involves taking out a financial instrument that offsets the position you have, so it cushions you, either partially or wholly, against losses.
- The organisation should have explicitly considered the use of hedging instruments to mitigate downside loss. Even if it ultimately decides not to incur the cost and effort of hedging, this decision should be discussed and recorded.
- The executive committee and board of the organisation should regularly review and discuss market risk positions.

The most commonly recognised metric for market risk is value at risk (VAR). This is a statistical method of modelling the likely amount of loss, given your current position, to a certain level of probability.

In addition to hedging strategies, you can reduce market risk by keeping debt within manageable levels, by matching your financing needs to your cash flows (so, for example, not using short-term finance for longer-term needs); by matching the currencies of your costs and expenses (so, for example, situating a factory in a country where you have a lot of revenue, so the costs offset some of the revenues); and by diversifying your investments and your supply chain (so you are not overly dependent on one supplier, for example).

# Developing a financial reporting risk framework

Directors of public companies are required to prepare an annual set of accounts (profit and loss accounts, balance sheet and cash flow statement, plus supporting notes) which present a "true and fair view" of the state of the company's affairs.

First-line responsibility sits with the CFO and finance department. This is then augmented by the third line, independent financial auditors, who provide an opinion on the company accounts. As CRO in the second line, your role is to provide check and challenge to the financial reporting risk controls that have been put in place.

Compressed timelines, external complexity, poor systems and overstretched staff can often make the financial reporting process stress-laden. It is also an area that has proven somewhat resistant to automation and systemisation – there are accounting systems, of course, but the consolidation exercise and the application of judgement still requires many hours of effort from skilled staff. It's a high-pressure exercise, and the consequences of failure are severe if accounts are late, have to be restated or if irregularities are found: fines, censure and reputational damage can result.

Good financial controls are therefore essential to navigating this area of activity and reducing risk. You should start with the following when developing a basic framework:

- Accountability and responsibility for financial reporting should be clearly defined.
- There should be a strong, adequately-resourced finance team, who are trained, developed, rewarded and motivated.
- There should be a culture of sound financial control and an understanding of finance throughout the organisation.
- Processes should be automated as far as possible in order to reduce errors and keep costs down.

- Well-documented policies and procedures should exist and be adhered to: it's especially important in the case of mergers and acquisitions that consistent accounting standards are applied across different entities, or any differences clearly noted.
- The finance team must keep up to date with evolving regulatory reporting requirements and ensure they are disseminated and operationalised.
- There should be a defined, repeatable process for monthly, quarterly and annual closing, reconciliations and adjustments to ensure consistency and reduce the probability of mistakes.
- The process should be reviewed and improved on an ongoing basis, using a learning mentality; where issues arise, a post-mortem review can try to prevent recurrence.
- A single, consistent chart of accounts should be applied across the organisation.
- Audit trails should exist for all reported information, whereby each significant number can be traced back and substantiated.
- An accounting system should perform repeatable tasks, such as regular and reversing accruals, consolidation and intercompany reconciliations.
- The system should provide analytical support and exception reporting to focus management attention on areas where there are anomalies, unusual patterns of spend, etc.

Deloitte[72] provides a useful reference for assessing the maturity of your financial reporting system. Looking at people, processes and technology, it recommends that you apply a maturity model analysis to these areas, identify areas for improvement and apply a project management mentality to both addressing weaknesses and to the monthly close process. Metrics such as time to close (the number of days post period end it takes to complete the accounts) and number of adjustments will provide an indication of the health of the financial reporting process.

## Summary

Financial risks are some of the most important, and visible, risks facing an organisation. When things go wrong in this space, they make the headlines. Having a good relationship with your CFO and a sound financial framework will go a long way to mitigating the risks and keeping the organisation on an even footing. With this risk addressed, we now dig further into the operational risks most organisations face, and how to protect against them.

# Chapter 10

*Operational risk*

Operational risk is defined as "*the risk of loss resulting from inadequate or failed internal processes, people and systems or from external events*".[73] In simple terms, it is to do with how things are accomplished and executed in a company. Here, it serves as the catch-all for all the non-strategic, non-people, non-financial and non-technical risks.

Depending on their nature, the ownership of some of these risks will vary. In general, however, most of these risks will come under the purview of the Chief Operating Officer (COO), if your organisation has one.

## Understanding operational risk

No single authoritative set of operational risks exists, and there will invariably be differences across industry sectors. Below, I have defined ten key subsets of operational risk, based on business experience. They refer to the risk of the organisation incurring loss due to the following:

- **Change management risk.** The risk that the organisation fails to respond to change or fails to execute needed changes in the organisation.

- **Financial crime risk.** The risk that the organisation is involved in money laundering, terrorist financing, bribery, corruption or sanctions breaches.
- **Fraud risk.** The risk that the organisation is a victim of internal or external fraudulent activities.
- **Legal risk.** The risk that the organisation fails to comply with the law or mismanages legal disputes.
- **Model risk.** The risk that data models used by the organisation fail to perform as expected, resulting in outcomes that are different to those expected.
- **Physical security risk.** The risk that the organisation's premises are unavailable, are breached or suffer loss or damage.
- **Product risk.** The risk that the organisation's products do not meet customer expectations.
- **Regulatory risk.** The risk that the organisation fails to meet its regulatory requirements.
- **Supplier/third-party risk.** The risk that the organisation's suppliers fail to meet their obligations.
- **Transaction processing risk.** The risk of errors in the organisation's core processing activities.

## Developing an operational risk framework

For each of the 10 risks, below I discuss how the risk might come about and suggest some of the commonly-deployed controls to manage them. Of course, you will have to tailor these to your organisational circumstances. I include these here to give you some prompts on controls to expect.

## Change management risk

Change is a constant in our working lives. However, how an organisation adapts to the changing external environment and mobilises its resources internally can be a key source of competitive advantage or disadvantage. Change management risk is the risk that the organisation fails to respond to change or fails to execute needed changes in the organisation. This is sometimes referred to as project risk.

To mitigate the risk of loss or failure in this space, a strong change management framework usually incorporates the following elements:

- Clarity within the organisation about what is changing, or needs to change, and why.
- Governance before launching into a new change – ensuring the organisation is prioritising the right things.
- A clear approach to change e.g. a chosen project-management methodology.
- Accountability for change i.e. who will ensure and "own" the success of the change project?
- Staff participation, including being consulted about the upcoming changes, being part of the change initiative and "owning" the embedding of the changes in day-to-day processes.
- Clear, repeated communications about what the change is about, how it relates to the strategy and the progress being made towards its goal.
- Priorities broken down into manageable components, with clear milestones and measures of success.
- Defined metrics which will indicate if the change has had the intended results.
- Celebration of success at each point along the way.

## Financial crime risk

Although this is a particular risk for financial services firms, it is also relevant for any firm that handles money or has financial dealings with counterparties. It includes the risk that the organisation has inadvertently laundered money from criminal activities or sanctioned countries or people. It also includes the risk of engaging in bribery or corruption. The reputational and financial consequences for noncompliance in this space are severe, and risk tolerance is usually extremely low.

Key controls to mitigate against financial crime include:

- An anti-money laundering policy and the appointment of a Money Laundering Risk Officer;
- Extensive "know your customer / know your business" procedures to identify the true identity of your customers, including checking with specialist third parties; this includes performing checks on individuals, directors of companies, the companies themselves and the countries in which they operate.
- Identity verification for individuals and validation of customer documentation; this is to ensure you are really dealing with the people/company they claim to be.
- Source of funds analysis to ensure it's clear where customers' funds are coming from; so, for example, if a customer is paying you for goods or services, or if they are depositing money with your organisation, has that money come from legitimate sources and can that be proven?
- An anti-bribery and corruption policy; stating the organisational position with regard to donations, gifts and entertainment and dealing with "politically exposed persons".
- Staff training and awareness, including how to identify suspicious behaviour.

## Fraud risk

Fraud risk can arise from internal sources such as employees, or external sources such as customers, hackers or the general public. Payroll fraud is an example of internal fraud where, for instance, an individual employee may falsely increase the amount they are paid. External fraud could be, for example, where a supplier bank account is wrongly changed and payment is sent to the wrong place. Key fraud controls include:

- Controls over payments, payroll, third-party setup and payment; this includes system limits, passwords, authentication and operational controls, such as "four-eyes" checks (see below).
- "Four-eyes" checks over sensitive transactions; this means that no one person is able to make a payment without a second person counter-signing it. Of course, even with this check, there is the possibility that two people collude, but you have reduced the risk somewhat by not allowing a sole actor to make a payment.
- Validation controls e.g. getting the customer to authenticate on an app before making a payment.
- Strong technology access controls and cyber controls; we covered this in the technology chapter.
- System reconciliations to identify discrepancies or irregularities.
- Audit trails; if people know that every action they take is attributed to their account, this is a powerful preventive control. It's also a detective control to identify what happened after the fact.
- A "layered" approach to security so that, in order to perpetuate a fraud, a person will have to circumnavigate several levels of system and people controls.
- Staff training and awareness, reinforced regularly. Anti-fraud certification schemes can help to raise awareness and also act as useful checklists – one good certification is the *Counter-fraud fundamentals* industry certification with IASME.[74]
- Rapid reporting and escalation of fraud events, with lessons learned quickly adopted.

- Removing the incentive for internal fraud, for example, by offering staff discounts to purchase company stock.

## Legal risk

Legal risk, where the organisation fails to comply with the law or mismanages legal disputes, can arise from a number of sources, including:

- **Commercial contracts.** The risk, for example, of financial loss or unintended consequences due to the use of a non-standard clauses in a contract, or clauses that leave loopholes open or weaken the organisation's position.
- **Intellectual property (IP) disputes**. This might involve the improper use of your own IP by somebody else, or the IP of another company being wrongly used by yours, resulting in legal disputes and financial loss.
- **Competition/antitrust law**. The risk of falling foul of stringent competition laws, the financial consequences of which can be enormous.
- **Employee relations.** The risk of employee action, either individual or collective, which disrupts your business and causes financial loss or reputational damage.
- **Litigation.** The risk of loss, or disruption to operations, through having legal action taken against you.
- **Tax law.** The risk of loss due to the tax treatment of your operations not being in line with expectations, or due to fines or reputational damage resulting from improper tax arrangements.

The best way to minimise legal risk is prevention – taking good advice, being aware of the legal space in which the organisation is operating, knowing the limits of what is acceptable and operating within that space. Having healthy and productive relationships with staff, customers, suppliers and regulators will provide a strong foundation as you will naturally avoid conflict that might lead to legal disputes.

Beyond that, legal risk can be reduced through the use of controls such as:

- Support from a strong in-house or external legal team;
- Standard contract terms and a good legal documentation system;
- The use of confidentiality and non-compete clauses in staff contracts to avoid individuals undertaking damaging activities, either during or after their employment;
- Reliable document storage mechanisms to avoid document leakage and loss; and
- Regular staff training and awareness on key legal topics facing the organisation.

## Model risk

Where an organisation uses models to aid in decision-making, this gives rise to risk because those models may not be accurate, executed appropriately or interpreted correctly. The key risks relating to model use are:

- **Data risk.** This is the risk that the data used to train the model is not accurate or not representative of the population it will be used on.
- **Systems risk.** The risk that the model is applied or implemented incorrectly.
- **Development risk.** This is the risk that the model was poorly or inaccurately trained.
- **Performance risk.** This is the risk that the model doesn't perform as expected or that performance degrades over time.

We discuss how to mitigate model risk in more detail in Chapter 14.

## Physical security risk

This area has changed more than most in very recent times. The advent of the serviced office, the move to cloud technology, the seismic shift to remote working, changing staff preferences, the desire for a new work-life balance and the decimation of international travel during the pandemic have all served to dramatically alter the physical office landscape. We have not yet settled into a new normal, post-Covid, but many believe it will be radically different from before. Nonetheless, the following provisions hold true for effective physical security risk management.

- A clear facilities management (FM) strategy is needed, linked to the overall goals of the organisation and optimising physical space and cost, both owned and leased.
- There should be clear assignment of ownership and responsibility for the FM strategy, ensuring there is sufficient internal and external expertise.
- Ongoing oversight of the real estate portfolio, including monitoring when leases are up for renewal and proactive suggestions on how to improve terms.
- A clear building maintenance schedule should be created, including evidence of compliance with all relevant building regulations, regulatory and statutory requirements.
- There should be a strong focus on financial management, governance and value for money in all FM dealings across the portfolio.
- Coordinated management and negotiation of all FM contracts.
- Implementation of facilities-related projects should be overseen by a competent executive – this will range from

acquisition and disposal to building refurbishments and to ongoing preventive maintenance.

- The buildings asset registers and the operating and maintenance manuals should be properly maintained for all properties owned.
- The building's internal environment should reflect the organisation's culture – collaborative, conservative, flexible, innovative or creative – to ensure that the space supports the organisational brand and vision.
- Facilities should be inclusive and accessible to all staff.
- Internal space should be optimised, through good planning, to ensure the organisation maximises value from the investment.
- To support the employee value proposition and be an attractive employer, buildings can contain further employee offerings such as gyms, canteens or retail space.
- There should be strong management of building security – both in terms of physical security and the resilience of power and utilities.
- Facilities changes should be communicated and managed in collaboration with staff to promote optimal acceptance and usage.
- Clear identification of facilities-related risks, from environmental to security, and the associated mitigation plans.
- Prompt, efficient service management, responding to employee requests and concerns relating to heat, light, ventilation, fire risks, etc. Employees are the eyes and ears of the organisation.
- Careful monitoring and reporting on facilities issues, health and safety issues, incidents and business continuity / disaster recovery planning and testing.

## Product risk

Product risk, the risk that the product will not meet customer expectations, has always existed, but it is amplified and accelerated in today's world. Where feedback can take place in seconds via social media and be seen by your whole customer base, it's not surprising that products and reputations live and die by how well product risk is managed.

While there are new, agile methods of product development which improve and shorten the product delivery cycle, certain principles still hold true, such as the need for stakeholder engagement, good design, sound development practices, quality assurance and structured launch plans. Whether the product is physical or virtual, product risk can be reduced (and product capability enhanced) by:

- knowing who your customer is and starting with their needs;
- understanding of the core capabilities of the organisation (and, just as importantly, what is non-core, so the organisation does not overreach);
- having a clear product roadmap, with regular, incremental and measurable benefits to each release and upgrade of the product;
- developing strong analytics showing how customers are accessing, buying and using your product;
- understanding when and why products are abandoned;
- holding a vibrant dialogue with your customer base;
- having a strong, repeatable methodology to define changes, develop, test, implement, learn and repeat;
- maintaining a well-organised and healthy product team and culture;
- ensuring you regularly take measures of customer satisfaction and respond to them; and

- having a rapid feedback loop for when things go wrong, and customer services teams who are empowered to make it right, first time, and quickly.

## Regulatory risk

Risk can arise in this space from noncompliance with either sector-specific rules or overarching requirements such as GDPR, or from the costs incurred in achieving regulatory compliance. Regulatory risk is often defined as relatively low likelihood but with severe impacts, such as censure, fines and restriction of business should it occur. Some key controls that help to avoid regulatory risk are:

- **Proactive risk identification, mapping and advisory**. Having a knowledgeable team identifying new trends and regulations and preparing the organisation to meet them, well in advance of their due dates.
- **In-built controls.** As far as is possible, building the controls needed to achieve compliance into the systems and processes of the organisation. So, for example, having strong "know your customer" checks built in to your customer onboarding system.
- **Response planning**. Dealing rapidly and decisively with the impact of compliance issues when they occur.
- **Strong regulatory relations**. Fostering a trusted relationship with your regulator, where you engage with them proactively and transparently, advise them early on of any issues and cooperate fully and transparently with enquiries.
- **Rule setting**. Clearly setting the internal boundaries for acceptable and unacceptable behaviour for staff, with reference to industry practice.

- **Training**. Defining the mandatory training that all employees must take, together with what declarations they need to sign, such as a code of conduct.
- **Prompt reporting**. Mandatory reporting, either on a periodic basis or in response to an incident.
- **A high-integrity culture**. Clear communication and reinforcement of where organisational boundaries lie.
- **Surveillance and detection of abuse**. In some sectors, such as financial services, compliance will play a technical surveillance role, monitoring trades for market abuse, conflicts of interest, etc.

## Supplier or third-party risk

Supplier/third-party risks occur when a supplier is unable to meet their obligations to you. Management of this risk is a broad and evolving topic, with issues such as Brexit and political upheaval complicating the landscape and creating supply chain disruption. To illustrate, roll-on-roll-off ferry traffic from Ireland to France increased sixfold in January 2021, while equivalent Dublin to Holyhead traffic halved. Organisations are having to be agile in switching up their logistics arrangements in order to manage cost and delivery risks.

We have also seen the importance of ensuring supply chains are abiding by laws and standards to avoid the horrific news reports of hauliers abusing or being abused by people traffickers. The Modern Slavery Act requires organisations to be aware of their supply chains and to ensure they are not contributing to this abuse. This is an area of significant risk, requiring sophisticated processes and systems to manage.

An effective supply chain management (SCM) strategy is required to mitigate against supplier risk. The SCM strategy should be aligned with the overall corporate strategy and adequately resourced to procure and distribute the organisation's products and services. It should include the following elements:

- **Accurate and careful scheduling and forecasting**. The organisation should take a forward-looking view of its resource requirements, forecasting future demand levels, building contingency and setting expectations with suppliers for what volumes will be required over the coming period.
- **Robust supplier management**. This includes all aspects of managing suppliers, from assessing and onboarding new suppliers, to dealing with non-performance, ethical or quality issues. It involves setting expectations for what the organisation wants from its suppliers, both quantitatively (volumes and prices) and qualitatively (quality, reliability and sustainability).
- **A defined tendering process**. This is needed to support the organisation for its more substantial purchases and should involve a fact-based process of researching the market, creating supplier long lists, designing and conducting the assessment process, defining the success criteria, evaluating suppliers and choosing the winning pitch.
- **Commercial negotiation**. This important step includes securing the best possible deals, including consideration of volumes, prices, discounts, pricing models, penalty clauses and securing other value-added services.
- **Supplier monitoring**. Ongoing relationships with suppliers must be overseen to ensure they're delivering maximum value and performing according to the standards and service levels that have been agreed upon.
- **Inventory management**. This is calculating how much is needed and when as well as how much stock to hold, thus minimising the costs of insurance, taxes, obsolescence and warehousing.

- **Safe and reliable transportation and logistics**. This includes managing appropriate and secure transportation of materials, using either in-house logistics staff or outsourced transportation specialists.
- **Environmental management**. Systems should be designed to prevent wastage, spillage and other incidents and, when these occur, they should be reported and dealt with.
- **Security and risk management**. Cargo should be appropriately secured at every step along the value chain to prevent fraud and theft.
- **Regular reporting**. Management should receive scheduled reports on suppliers, costs, volumes and incidents.

## Transaction processing risk

Deutsche Bank defines transaction processing risk as: *"The risk that deficiencies in transaction processing or in our internal processes or controls result in losses. The risk is caused by human error, IT applications system failure and inadequate process design."*[75] This risk can be exacerbated by disjointed systems, manual processing, poor data management methodologies or staff changes.

Transaction processing controls include:

- A comprehensive quality assurance strategy at the point of implementing new systems, including testing all foreseeable transactions and combinations;
- Documented charts of accounts and systems flow charts that are understood by staff;
- Clear, documented processes for data entry, reconciliation, exception management and reporting;
- Staff expertise and training; and
- System reconciliations and rapid exception reporting.

Better design and fewer, more modern and more agile systems will ultimately reduce this risk.

## Summary

There is no one-size-fits-all set of controls that can be blindly applied to your organisation. This is where there's no substitute for your knowledgeable, experienced first-line staff, prompted by the risk team, considering their processes, their weaknesses and how to improve them. However, hopefully the above serves as a useful checklist against which to benchmark your controls.

This completes our assessment of our pyramid of 20 risks. Ensuring you have robust controls in place across all these areas provides a great foundation for you as CRO. Depending on the maturity of your organisation, getting all of these areas to a good level of risk management will be an endeavour in itself. However, I have kept one even more fundamental risk to the end – sustainability risk.

# Chapter 11

## Sustainability risk

Although it doesn't form part of the risk pyramid above, it would be remiss not to include possibly the greatest ultimate risk we face – sustainability risk. This is a newly emerging risk area that incorporates environmental and social responsibility and one that is gaining a lot of traction in the face of climate change and other social developments.

According to a study by KPMG[76], 51% of banks assigned responsibility for climate risk to the CEO, and 37% to the CRO. Some organisations choose to appoint a Chief Sustainability Officer (CSO). Whether or not a CSO exists, the CRO is a key person responsible for identifying, managing and monitoring sustainability-related risks.

> *"I would argue that a CRO is one of the few senior executives able to look across the breadth of ESG and sustainability issues and bring together cross-functional teams to address them, with an eye to leveraging business opportunities and managing threats."*

> *The Risk Coalition*[77]

## ESG vs. Sustainability

ESG stands for environment, social and governance and is rapidly being adopted by financial institutions as a framework for assessing these areas. While environment and climate are the topics that are usually at the top of most minds, the fuller scope of ESG comprises the following:

- Environmental: greenhouse gases, carbon emissions, supply chain, operational emissions, financed emissions, waste management;
- Social: diversity, equity and inclusion, staff relations, community involvement;
- Governance: the composition of the board, involvement of wider stakeholder groups.

Sustainability takes a broader remit and has been defined as "Meeting the needs of the present without compromising the ability of future generations to meet their own needs".[78]

However your organisation refers to it, and whatever the industry you work in, sustainability and ESG will become increasingly relevant to your organisation and, as CRO, you need to set the tone for the organisational response.

## Understanding sustainability risk

The Federation of European Risk Management Associations (FERMA) defines sustainability risk as an *"uncertain social or environmental event or condition that, if it occurs, can cause significant negative impact on the company. It also includes the opportunity that may be available to an organisation because of changing social or environmental factors".*[79] In simple terms, it refers to the risks of continuing organisational activities which are not sustainable. Thus, a sustainability risk framework aims to align a company's financial goals with its long-term viability.

*"We're in business to save our home planet"*
*Patagonia*

Climate change events are increasingly being felt across the world. There is a growing sense that we cannot continue to overextend our planet's capabilities. In his latest book, *A Life on Our Planet*, David Attenborough outlines a dystopian but sadly realistic scenario for 2100: a catastrophic loss of biodiversity and empty, polluted oceans, passing a tipping point from which we cannot recover.[80] This is already being felt in the UK through increasingly regular floods and in the US and Australia with increased storm damage, blistering summers and forest fires. We've seen the polar ice caps melting at an alarming rate and, if we don't prevent this process from continuing, the consequences from sea levels rising will be devastating. On the social front, the surge in the Black Lives Matter movement and the LGBTQ+ agenda, as well as the recognition of mental health issues, show the demand for change in the world.

Progressive organisations are working to re-examine their agendas, to work with the planet and bring back nature's natural defences. In Ireland, the authority previously known for harvesting peat has completely re-oriented its mission to protecting the remaining bogland. The forest agency, Coillte, is replanting indigenous trees. Rewilding experiments such as at Knepp reserve in the UK show that nature is much better at building flood defences than humans are.

These examples are not that far removed from the world of corporates and finance either. Banks are coming under pressure to stop funding projects which kill biodiversity or continue emitting vast amounts of carbon; insurance companies have to take on board a whole new range of risks, from pandemic cover to catastrophic damage due to weather events, and customers and investors, particularly millennials, are mobilising to move their business away from big companies which do not appear to be prioritising sustainability. All of this tells us that putting sustainability at the core of your organisation's mission will also contribute to the sustainability of your organisation. If we are to have longevity, we need to take account of sustainability topics and act accordingly.

ESG may also have an impact on whether you can secure investment to grow your company. Investment companies such as BlackRock are increasing their scrutiny of the organisations they invest in, expecting them to take measure such as:

- Publishing a "temperature alignment metric" for their public equity and bond funds;
- Incorporating climate considerations into capital markets assumptions (for example, looking at the impact of climate regulation on long term cash flows);
- Implementing a "heightened-scrutiny model" in their active portfolios as a framework for managing holdings that pose significant climate risk (including flagging holdings for potential exit);
- Launching investment products with explicit temperature alignment goals, including products aligned to a "net zero" pathway; and
- Using their significant influence to ensure that the companies their clients are invested in are both mitigating climate risk and considering the opportunities presented by a transition to being "net zero".

As Larry Fink said in his 2021 letter to CEOs, "*I believe that the pandemic has presented such an existential crisis – such a stark reminder of our fragility – that it has driven us to confront the global threat of climate change more forcefully and to consider how, like the pandemic, it will alter our lives. It has reminded us how the biggest crises, whether medical or environmental, demand a global and ambitious response."*[81]

Climate risks are sometimes grouped into two categories: physical risk and transition risk. Physical risk considers damage due to climate change, such as flood risk. Transition risk covers the impact on revenues of transitioning away from certain industries, such as oil and gas production, or the cost of meeting new requirements, such as improving building efficiency.

It's important to remember that transition risks pose opportunities in financial services also – customers will need financing in order to make their buildings more energy efficient, to transition to newer machinery, etc. The market for green finance is large and growing.

## Industry standards

There is a huge range of international standards and laws around the environment and sustainability that can guide your creation of a sustainability risk framework and feed into your understanding of best practice. Below is a (by no means complete) list of the standards, bodies and regulation covering this growing space.

- **ISO 14000** is a set of international standards covering environmental performance that encourages reduction of environmental damage and compliance with environmental laws and regulations.
- The **Equator Principles**, specific to project finance, are *"a financial industry benchmark for determining, assessing and managing environmental and social risk in projects"*.[82]
- The **Sustainable Development Goals**[83] are a list of 17 goals agreed as part of the Paris accord in 2015. They cover a range of targets, ranging from clean water to equality, education to clean energy.

- The **Task Force on Climate-Related Financial Disclosures (TCFD)** by the **Financial Stability Board**, updated in 2021, is now mandatory in the UK and has four pillars: governance, strategy, risk management and metrics and targets.
- The **Sustainability Accounting Standards Board (SASB)** is a non-profit organisation which has developed sustainability reporting standards across 77 industries, aiming to promote transparency and comparability between organisations.
- The **International Sustainability Standards Board** was formed at COP26 in Glasgow and is tasked with developing sustainability disclosure standards to meet the needs of investors. The SASB standards above are now consolidated to sit under the ISSB, which is part of the IFRS foundation.
- The **Sustainable Finance and Disclosure Regulation (SFDR)** imposes mandatory ESG disclosure obligations for asset managers and other financial markets participants within the EU.
- **EU Taxonomy.**[84] The EU has a huge range (over 500 directives, regulations and decisions) of environmental laws. The EU taxonomy is a classification system, establishing a list of environmentally sustainable economic activities.
- The **EU Corporate Sustainability Reporting Directive**, under review at time of writing, is expanding its scope to mid-size companies, and adding topics such as strategy, governance and resilience, widening the stakeholder group and adding forward-looking information. It already covered environmental protection, social responsibility and treatment of employees, respect for human rights, anti-corruption and bribery and company board diversity.

- The European Finance Reporting Advisory Group is preparing **European Sustainability Reporting Standards (ESRS)**.
- The **US Securities and Exchange Commission (SEC)** has issued proposed climate reporting rules as of March 2022, requiring disclosures in company 10-Ks and registration documents for companies planning to float. In addition, it is proposing associated audit and attestation requirements.
- The UK Government's updated **Streamlined Energy and Carbon Reporting** requirements build on previous reporting requirements and aim to encourage adoption of energy-efficiency measures for more UK companies.
- From a legal standpoint, in the UK, the **Environmental Protection Act 1990** defines the duty of care of all "waste producers" to manage their waste safely and responsibly.[85] Noncompliance is a criminal offence and carries punitive fines. In England and Wales, regulation is enforced by the Environment Agency.
- In Australia, the **National Greenhouse and Energy Reporting Act** imposes reporting requirements on qualifying companies around their greenhouse gas emissions, energy consumption and production activities to the regulator.
- **B-Corp** is non-profit organisation dedicated to *"transforming the global economy to benefit all people, communities, and the planet"*. Organisations can sign up to their wide-ranging standards and be accredited as a B-Corp company.
- The **Network for Greening the Financial System** is a body which analyses a range of climate scenarios, from orderly to disorderly to the grim-sounding "hothouse world" scenario.

- **Global Reporting Initiative (GRI) reporting.** The GRI sets sustainability reporting standards covering economic, environmental and social topics.

This veritable alphabet soup of organisations and regulation creates a daunting list of overlapping requirements. In fact, according to Aberdeen Standard Investments, globally, there has been a 72% increase in ESG-related legislation or guidelines since 2013.[86] To try to address this, five organisations – CDP, the Climate Disclosure Standards Board (CDSB), the Global Reporting Initiative (GRI), the International Integrated Reporting Council (IIRC) and the Sustainability Accounting Standards Board (SASB), have co-authored a single vision[87] for sustainability reporting, which also aligns with the TCFD requirements. Interestingly, it specifically calls for reporting around risk management within its content. In addition, the ISSB and SEC are adopting the TCFD pillars in their disclosure requirements.

## Linkage to other risks

Climate and sustainability risks do not exist in a vacuum – they impact and are impacted by other risks. It's important to model with your management team what the impacts could be for your organisation, but, for example, most companies will want to consider:

- Strategic risk: what lines of business and markets may become less viable due to climate and social changes? What products will become redundant if not updated? What new lines of business and investments should be considered to lean into the future?
- Financial risk: in particular, credit risk (if natural disasters will impact on customers' ability to repay their debts) and financial reporting risk (failing to comply with increasingly

onerous reporting regulation, or being accused of "greenwashing"). In addition, failure (or inability) to insure against catastrophic events could lead to financial losses.

- Operational risks: including physical security (due to natural disasters and temperature change), product risk (e.g. if you are in manufacturing and need to change your products to be less carbon-intensive), regulatory risk and supplier risk (e.g. if your supply chain is affected by climate matters).

- Counterparty risk: severe events and natural disasters could impact on customers and counterparties, disrupting their business and affecting their ability to repay, thus increasing your expected credit losses (ECLs)

## Developing a sustainability risk framework

This area is a moving feast and requirements are continuing to evolve. Staying on top of developments and working with other stakeholders to shape requirements will be important. At a minimum, you need to consider:

- Your organisation's climate strategy, including its own operational emissions, carbon offsets for travel, financed emissions (if it is a lender), sustainable finance (e.g. financing clean energy generation) and investments in new technology and innovation to tackle climate issues.

- Governance, roles and responsibilities – who will set the targets, take responsibility for execution and oversee it?

- Financial reporting – disclosures on the organisation's impact on climate, both in the up-front "glossy" part of the financial statements, and in the body of the accounts.

- The CRO in particular will need to consider climate risk management and its impact on other related risks, including credit and financial risks.

- Metrics and targets for the organisation, both in terms of its own operational footprint and emissions, and if it is a lender, on its financed emissions.

It's also important to consider how to tie management incentives to climate-related performance. According to KPMG[88], 51% of banks surveyed were linking remuneration to climate metrics and targets.

## Good to great

However, beyond the desire to achieve compliance with emerging regulation, to really embrace the changes that are happening, I believe you have to look deeper at what it takes to become a truly sustainable operation. Below I have listed what I feel are the tenets of a truly strong sustainability risk framework. I have loosely based it on Patagonia's blueprint, from their 40 years of operating as one of the most admired and sustainable organisations in the world.[89] While not every organisation will attain the levels below, they set a bar to which others can aspire.

- The very mission of the organisation should speak to doing some degree of good in the world. This does not mean that you need to be an "eco" organisation – software companies which make lives easier, pharma companies which produce vaccines and supermarket chains which ensure food security all perform a fundamental social good. Even the much-maligned banks provide necessary infrastructure funding for wind farms, roads, bridges and hospitals. What's key is how they go about it.
- The organisation should fundamentally believe in treating its employees well. This means (mostly) permanent roles with pensions, benefits and maternity leave. Childcare, shared parental leave, flexible, hybrid working and a trust-based

approach are even better.

- The organisation should foster a culture of trust, wellbeing, transparency and open dialogue. It should not cover up dissent.
- The organisation should have visibility up and down its supply chain and continuously monitor it to ensure its sources are ethical, based on fair trade, a working wage and non-exploitation.
- The organisation should do all it can to source materials which are sustainable. It should work with its suppliers to constantly improve and should swap out better materials whenever they can, even when this costs more.
- The organisation should have a waste management strategy, reducing waste as far as possible, and favouring recyclable and recycled materials.
- The organisation should push back against one-dimensional expectations of ever-increasing quarter-on-quarter financial performance in favour of shared growth, product innovation and sustainability. Think this is unrealistic? Read Paul Polman's book *Net Positive* to see what was done at Unilever to address the culture of short-termism.
- The organisation should report on its sustainability efforts, avoiding superficial "greenwashing" and taking care to be just as transparent about areas in which it can do better as about its successes.
- The organisation's physical spaces (offices, factories, etc.) should be designed or upgraded to be energy-efficient, sustainable and human-friendly places.[90]

## How banks are addressing climate risk

As lenders, banks have an additional responsibility – to think about the impact of the activities they finance. As responsible lenders, it is increasingly expected that banks understand their financed emissions, and other impacts of their loan books. Common practices now include:

- Adding ESG considerations to their on-boarding and due diligence exercises;
- Asking customers for more information up front about the purpose of lending, and specifically whether it is contributing to, or guarding against, climate change or social good;
- Changing credit policies about what lines of business they will and will not lend to;
- Scoring loans on a scale from green to brown, and charging more for more polluting activities (and less for carbon-reducing activities);
- Performing additional due diligence in carbon-intensive sectors; and
- Seeking to offload loans that no longer meet the newer green standards.

The transition will be challenging to organisations of all types. The scale of the issue is enormous, but change is possible. For an example about what is possible, read the case study below about how one of the biggest organisations in the world, in an industry that produces a lot of waste, is changing how it operates.

## Case study: The NHS

The NHS is a great example of an organisation that has embraced sustainability as a goal. The NHS is the fourth biggest organisation in the world, and one of the greatest users and consumers of the earth's resources. It represents a quarter of the UK public sector's carbon emissions. Global healthcare emissions are of such magnitude that if it were a country, it would be the fifth biggest emitter. Therefore, providing healthcare is paradoxically harming population health through environmental effects. This is both directly through fires, floods and "heat domes" and indirectly through crop failure, soil erosion and famines, droughts, emerging and recurrent infectious diseases such as viral pandemics (Ebola, SARS, MERS, Covid) and natural animal habitat degradation.

If the environmental impact of providing healthcare is not managed well, it will only increase the demands placed upon the system itself, leading to further emissions and creating a negative feedback loop. It is firmly within the healthcare industry's interests to deal with its environmental footprint.

This existential threat has been recognised at executive and grassroot levels throughout the organisation and is gaining momentum. Despite the pressures of increasing chronic diseases, an ageing population, increased patient demand, the budget crisis and the Covid pandemic, the NHS is addressing environmental sustainability more seriously than it ever has. Below are just some of the initiatives they have put in place:

-   Greener NHS has been set up as part of NHS England, with the UK's first Chief Sustainability Officer appointed in 2020, with clear operative direction and key deliverables outlined for organisations. Since 2007, its health and social care carbon footprint has reduced by 18%, which equates in scale to the annual emissions from a small country such as Mauritius or Cyprus.

- A full environmental impact assessment of the carbon and water footprint of health and social care in England was undertaken to allow meaningful management of its emissions.
-   Hospital trusts are declaring climate emergencies.
-   Trusts are publishing sustainable development management plans, which aim to tackle the environmental footprint in their organisations.
-   Scope 1, 2 and 3 emissions have reduction targets. These include direct and indirect emissions, building and construction,

procurement and supply chain, pharmaceuticals and medical equipment supply. Engineers, clinicians, procurement and industry are working together to achieve these.

- "Carbon hotspots" as identified in assessments are targeted first, with national and local directives, whilst maintaining patient safety and clinical efficacy, e.g.

  - Targets for reductions in Desflurane use, an anaesthetic gas which is 2,540 times more warming for the planet than carbon dioxide. Many hospitals have removed it entirely from their drug formulary.
  - 3% of NHS emissions come from metered dose inhalers for conditions such as asthma, and these are being changed to the non-polluting dry powder inhalers, which are just as efficacious.
  - Plastic reduction pledges have been put in place.
  - There has been investment and procurement in green innovation and products that exist within the circular economy.
  - Greener travel has been enabled for staff, which will improve local air quality and staff health e.g. cycling training schemes and reducing unnecessary patient visits via one-stop clinics, virtual consultations and examination of transport fleets.

- Green care pathways and green low-carbon prescribing have been put in place, improving population health and thereby reducing demands for health interventions along the entire patient journey.[91]

If the behemoth that is the NHS can make changes of this magnitude, so can we all.

## Summary

Nelson Mandela said *"everything seems impossible until it is done"*. While there may be short term trade-offs between financial performance and ESG, the long-term viability of your organisation depends on you finding the right balance and addressing sustainability, now. In the *Harvard Business Review* article, 'Lessons from Companies That Put Purpose Ahead of Short-Term Profits', Andrew White says: *"The outcome of this process is not a polished statement of purpose - but significant decisions grounded in a deep understanding of purpose characterized by a quiet sense of service to something greater than the immediate needs of customers and short-term demands of investors."*[92]

It's obvious that the time of sustainability is here. It's mainstream, it's good business and it's necessary. This is our greatest risk and our ultimate act of stewardship. As CRO, if you're not managing this risk, how much do the others really matter?

# Chapter 12

*Creating a control strategy*

A generally-accepted approach to managing risk includes the following steps:

- Identify the risk;
- Assess it;
- Manage it (see below); and
- Report it.

The preceding chapters discuss the identification and assessment of risks. Once you have set out your risk appetite and identified your key risks, it's time to consider what actions the organisation needs to take to address them. There are multiple approaches to dealing with risk. You can:

- terminate or avoid the risk altogether i.e. don't undertake the activity (product launch, venturing into a new market) that is giving rise to the risk;
- control the risk to bring it within tolerance;
- transfer or outsource the risk e.g. through insurance;
- mitigate or reduce the risk e.g. through a hedging strategy; or
- tolerate and accept the risk as part of being in business.

Where management has considered the risks and decided to proceed with the activity, well-designed and executed controls are the key tool to keep those risks under control. As I said in Chapter 5, inherent risk minus these controls equals residual risk. The aim is to get this residual risk to within the defined risk appetite. This control strategy will be the core part of your risk framework: the basis of your organisation's risk management approach. In creating it, we need to use judgement to satisfy the needs of the organisation while remaining vigilant.

> *"Selecting the most appropriate risk treatment option(s) involves balancing the potential benefits derived in enhancing the achievement of objectives against the costs, efforts or disadvantages of proposed actions. Justification for the design of risk treatments and the operation of internal control is broader than solely economic considerations and should take into account all of the organisation's obligations, commitments and stakeholder views."[93]*

We have explored many different types of risk control in the previous chapters, but here I'll outline the overarching strategic approaches to setting those controls that will enable you to take consistent and thoughtful action.

## Types of control

When designing a set of controls to manage risks, it helps to consider the different types of control that exist and how they work together to build up a defence.

- **Directive controls** are set by management. Policies set out what limits and approaches should be taken and should cover all major areas of the organisation, including people, legal and operations. Procedures explain how it is done, operationalising the intended controls. See the

Appendix for a sample set of policies and procedure types.

- **Pervasive controls.** This includes training, policies and procedures, segregation of duties and incentives. These form an overlay of controls that create an environment and culture less conducive to the risk occurring. However, they are not, in and of themselves, sufficient to prevent risks occurring.

- **Preventive controls.** As the name suggests, these types of controls exist to stop the risk occurring in the first place. Examples are system controls preventing unauthorised users accessing them, limits (for example on spending) and physical security gates.

- **Detective controls.** These controls tell us when something has gone wrong. Examples are burglar alarms, exception reports and alerts. They are an important part of the control environment as they don't allow mistakes and problems to fall through the net, but they need to be paired with other, preventive controls as they only kick in after the event has happened.

## The role of insurance

Insurance is a critical element of the organisation's risk response. Through contracts with insurance companies, it allows the organisation to transfer risk outside of the organisation in return for the payment of risk premiums. Some types of insurance are mandatory for the sector; others are optional and there can be a genuine organisational debate about the merits of paying for insurance vs. self-insuring. Responsibility for insurance usually sits with the COO or CFO.

Key types of insurance to expect in most organisations include:

- Directors and officers ("D&O") insurance
- Professional indemnity ("PII") insurance

- Buildings insurance
- Plant and machinery insurance
- Contents insurance
- Employer's liability insurance
- Public liability insurance
- Product liability insurance
- Fraud insurance
- Cybersecurity insurance
- Business interruption insurance
- Credit risk insurance
- Key man insurance

Insurance cover, and its adequacy and value for money, should be subject to regular discussion and review, at both executive and board level.

## The three lines of defence

To better understand the relationship that the CRO has with key stakeholders in the context of risk, we can look to operational risk theory. This states there are three lines of defence an organisation has to combat risk.

- **First line**. This is the business management of the organisation. As the owners of the business lines, they are also the owners of the risks associated with their businesses. They are primarily responsible for identifying and resolving the risks that endanger their business goals.
- **Second line**. These are the control functions in the organisation, including the CRO (you), legal and compliance. They define the frameworks that the organisation should operate under and provide critical "check and challenge" to the first line. They are not considered to "own" any risks themselves.

- **Third line**. This is the independent audit line. These are people not directly connected with the organisation who review its actions against its goals, policies and procedures. Typically, you have external audit, provided by a specialist third-party firm, and internal audit, who are employees of the organisation but have a separate reporting line to the rest of the business.

## What makes a good control?

Not all controls are created equal. The following are a few rules of thumb, which *generally* apply:

- A preventive control is superior to a detective control: Preventing something happening in the first place is usually preferable to finding out about it after the fact and having to fix it as well as the fallout it's created.
- A system control is generally better than a human control: As long as it is well-defined and properly executed, system controls are capable of monitoring and preventing risks as well as highlighting exceptions, ceaselessly and consistently, 24-7. Humans are an indispensable part of the risk framework, but they are better suited to more varied, complex, nuanced tasks which require judgement.
- Layering of controls provides greater protection: A combination of a preventive control plus a detective control provides a rigorous approach, as long as each control performs a distinct function. This can, however, be taken to excess and lead to unnecessary, redundant controls which can slow an organisation down. If a preventive control is truly 100% effective, and can be proven to be so, then avoid piling on other controls just for the sake of it. Trust the process.
- In-built controls are better than those added later: Built-in strength and resilience usually beats checks layered on top, after the fact. Good design is the best control.

A number of risk systems now offer control "libraries" which allow you to assess your controls and even benchmark yourself against other organisations. I discuss some of these in Chapter 12.

When considering the strength of a control, it's important to consider two dimensions:

1) How well-designed is the control in the first place? Can it be relied upon to prevent or detect problems? With what certainty? Are there loopholes? Are there incorrect assumptions that have been made about its operation, or about the risks that could occur?
2) How well is the control operating? It may be designed perfectly, but for any number of reasons, including human error, bad training or incorrect implementation, it might not be operating as planned.

When risks occur, it helps to look at what failed, whether it's design or operation, to ensure the right remedial action is taken. This learning loop is essential to strengthening the control environment and ensuring the same mistake never happens twice.

## Tools to support your control framework

There are several strategic tools which are invaluable as a CRO and which will support your control framework.

### Policies and procedures

Policies set out what limits and approaches should be taken. Procedures explain how it is done, operationalising the intended controls. Policies should cover all major areas of the organisation, from people to legal to operations. See the Appendix for a sample set of policies and procedures as a starting point for most organisations.

## Risk and controls self-assessment (RCSA)

The RCSA is an essential risk tool and the primary way in which the first line assesses its control environment. An RCSA should answer the following questions:

- What are the key risks that this department faces?
- How great is the inherent risk of this occurring (i.e. before controls are considered)?
- What are the controls that prevent, mitigate or reduce this risk?
- Are they well designed?
- Are they operating effectively?
- Do these controls bring the residual risk (i.e. after controls are considered) to within the organisation's risk appetite?
- If not, what more could be done to strengthen the controls?
- Who will take on these additional actions?
- By when will these actions be completed?

*Why RCSAs fall short of the mark*
When done thoughtfully and well, an RCSA is a powerful tool which forces management to step back and critically assess their area. However, all too often, they can become laundry lists of every conceivable little thing and degenerate into enormous spreadsheets in 4pt font, where you can no longer see the wood from the trees. Management then starts to view them as a painful compliance tick-box exercise of little value.

In order to ensure the RCSA process is valuable, CROs should ensure that:

- the process kicks off with a thoughtful evaluation of the big-picture risks facing the department, area or organisation;
- the RCSA focuses on areas of key risk and doesn't waste time on small, obscure issues. Know when to stop. There is

undoubtedly an 80/20 rule at play here in that 80% of your effort will uncover the key risks of interest. Focus on the major areas of risk and don't devalue the process by sweating the smaller stuff;

- there is sufficient discussion and peer review to make the process meaningful and to interrogate and challenge the first-line logic of business managers. Your business colleagues are not necessarily programmed to think about risk. It's not their core skill, and so we should not expect them to perform this task well in a vacuum. A thoughtful and engaging conversation which asks questions such as, "Have you considered what would happen if X occurred?" can make the process much more meaningful; and

- they entertain the widest view of risk. A concern about speed to market or product irrelevance is just as valid as a concern about accuracy or completeness.

Finally, an RCSA should pass the "reasonableness" test. At the end of the day, the outstanding risk areas should mirror the things that keep the manager awake at night. If not, it needs to be looked at again.

## Operational risk indicators

To monitor how your risk controls are performing and the risk level of the company, it is common to define a set of operational risk indicators. These measures provide an indication of where risk could be better managed.

When defining this set of measures, it's important to include lead as well as lag indicators – the early measures that will provide some advance warning of a brewing problem, rather than those that tell you after the fact. For example, waiting for the number of customer complaints to go up is a poor way of finding out about dissatisfaction. It would be preferable to also look at volume of calls to the call centre, anecdotal feedback from customer services, Trustpilot and App Store reviews, and, of course, data analytics on your website, social channels and applications. In this way, you can find out where your customers are going, getting frustrated and checking out, and take remedial action ahead of time.

See the Appendix for a starting list of operational risk indicators, which will need to be tailored to your organisation.

## Summary

Your control framework is your protection against risks. Good design is a matter of science – sound, sensible, well-designed, appropriate controls, matched to the genuine risks faced, are key. However, the art is in focusing on the risks that really matter and in designing the best, most efficient and effective controls that don't hamper the organisation. Plus, of course, you need the right oversight and governance, which is where we turn to next.

# Chapter 13

*Governance and oversight*

Effective risk management requires a governance framework, so that if the proverbial tree falls in the forest, there is someone to hear it, understand the consequences, ensure lessons are learned and that follow-up actions take place. Ideally, of course, to also have the wisdom to predict, and prevent, the tree falling in the first place!

*"Risk governance refers to the institutions, rules conventions, processes and mechanisms by which decisions about risks are taken and implemented."*[94]

Independent oversight is one of the core tenets of good business practice. Having a set of people, independent from the day-to-day execution, to provide expert opinion, challenge thinking and hold executive leaders to account is fundamental to the operation of successful organisations.

As far as governance relates to risk, the Corporate Governance Council states that risk governance:

- is the architecture within which risk management operates in a company;

- defines the way in which a company undertakes risk management; and
- provides guidance for sound and informed decision-making and elective allocation of resources.[95]

As CRO, it is your responsibility to ensure that your organisation has sound governance, both over the organisation as a whole, and over its risk management practices.

## Leadership and forums

Governance is ultimately the responsibility of an organisation's board. They must work with executive management to define the risk appetite of the organisation and approve the systems, policies and processes by which that risk management appetite will be managed. The board is expected, through analysis and enquiry, to satisfy themselves that management is discharging its responsibilities effectively.

Depending on the size of the organisation, the board may set up subsidiary committees, such as an audit committee or risk committee, to help discharge its duties. These committees may contain a subset of the board members, plus perhaps some other external experts. They have the right and the responsibility to escalate significant matters back to the main board for consideration. The roles and responsibilities of these committees will need to be clearly defined by the main board.

In a PricewaterhouseCoopers (PwC) blog, they argue that *"the supporting committee structure is essential to the effective oversight and monitoring of this model. Key to the success of these committees is a set of clearly defined terms of reference, committee membership and reporting requirements."*[96]

The terms of reference define what the committee is responsible for, how often it meets, its scope, attendance, frequency etc.

It should be clear what functions the board has delegated to it. Committee membership defines the attendees, quorum and voting rights. Reporting requirements lay out what the board expects from its subcommittee, and at what frequency.

Depending on the size of the organisation, you may need to add layers of meetings below the committee level in order to cover the ground required. For example, you could schedule the following:

- A risk and audit committee meeting at board level quarterly to discuss the high-level risk issues.
- A risk management meeting at management level at monthly intervals to gather data for the risk and audit committee.
- Ad hoc meetings on more specialist risk subjects, such as cybersecurity or quality assurance. These would feed into the risk management meetings.

## Sample risk committee agenda

If you need to create a risk committee agenda, the below is a helpful skeleton that you can build around. I like to have a standing agenda like this, which also allows sufficient time for the specialist deep dives and thematic reviews that often yield the more interesting insights.

- o Executive summary;
- o Horizon scanning and recent external events;
- o Overview of key organisational risks (focusing on those sitting near or above risk appetite);
- o Risk event report (how many, what happened, what was the cost/impact, what actions are being progressed as a result);
- o First line of defence assurance reports (what reviews were carried out in the past period, what were the results and learnings, any remedial actions required);

- o Third line of defence audit reports (audits completed in the last period and their findings, plus the schedule of upcoming audits);
- o Outstanding actions review (showing how well the organisation is completing the remedial actions it previously committed to); and
- o Specialist thematic deep dives (covering detailed technical areas such as cybersecurity, model risk etc.).

The role of the risk committee is to inform the board and allow them oversight of the risk management process but also to seek its counsel on critical topics. It's therefore important to leave enough time and space to debate these. It's very powerful to ask the board, especially those who are independent and don't work in the organisation every day, what their views are, where they think your blind spots are and what issues you are over-worrying or under-worrying about. This much needed perspective can be lost unless you actually take the time to ask this senior group what they think. It's all too common to have the main agenda and presentation taking up 59 minutes of the hour, with a perfunctory "Any questions?" at the end – this is a wasted opportunity. I suggest that at least a third to a half of the time available is allotted to discussion rather than presentation. This also assumes that papers have been submitted to the committee members sufficiently in advance, so they have had time to read, prepare and think.

## Policies and procedures

A risk framework document should set the overall context for risk management in the organisation. It should include roles and responsibilities, the three lines of defence, the set of policies and arrangements for assurance, monitoring and reporting.

Cascading from that, you need a robust and up-to-date set of policies that prescribe the organisation's approach to all key areas of governance. These should be supported by documented procedures for all key processes. They usually cover the areas of finance, people, operations, technology, legal, compliance, sales and marketing. A sample checklist of policies is included in the Appendix.

## Supervisory framework and regulations

While a detailed overview of supervisory topics pertaining to all industries is beyond the scope of this book, below I cover some key considerations for financial services, which is my area of expertise. In the UK, financial services organisations are regulated by the Financial Conduct Authority and the Prudential Regulation Authority. Below is a small selection of regulations that are relevant, at the time of writing, in a financial services context.

### Market Abuse Regulation (MAR)

The EU MAR was brought in in 2016 and transferred into UK legislation post-Brexit. It *"aims to increase market integrity and investor protection, enhancing the attractiveness of securities markets for capital raising"*,[97] and contains prohibitions on insider dealing, unlawful disclosure of inside information and market manipulation and provisions to prevent and detect these.

### Senior Management Certification Regime (SMCR)

The SMCR, introduced in 2016, applies to senior managers of the organisation and seeks to achieve greater individual accountability when things go wrong in regulated organisations. It tries to avoid the possibility of decisions being made by committee and everybody was responsible (so nobody was responsible). The

SMCR requires organisations to define clear responsibilities and allocate them to named individuals. It also defines certain "controlled functions", which again are allocated to individual people.

Some of the key controlled functions include:

- CF 1 Director function;
- CF 2 Non-Executive Director function;
- CF 3 Chief Executive function; and
- CF10 Compliance oversight function.[98]

The CRO occupies the SMF4 function. If misconduct occurred in a particular area and the named individual responsible for that area did not demonstrate steps that they would be reasonably expected to take, then the FCA is able to take action against that individual, including fines, censure and bans on doing business.

## The FCA's conduct rules

The conduct rules defined by the FCA state that all employees working in regulated entities must:

- Act with integrity;
- Act with due care, skill and diligence;
- Be open and cooperative with the FCA, the PRA and all regulators;
- Pay due heed to the interests of customers and treat them fairly; and
- Observe proper standards of market conduct.

Failure to observe the conduct rules can lead to unlimited fines, censure and suspensions or bans on doing business.[99]

## GDPR

As mentioned in Chapter 8, the General Data Protection Regulation (GDPR), rolled out in 2016 (a busy year for regulation!), sets out a number of consumer rights and protections relating to their data.

## The role of assurance

Assurance is, put simply, the way in which management gets comfort that the risk controls it intended for the organisation to put in place are operating and doing so effectively. Gaining assurance is the responsibility of the first line, i.e. the business itself. It cannot be delegated to the risk function. Risk functions will, however, review and provide challenge to management on whether the assurance performed is sufficient.

Examples of assurance controls are:

- Listening to samples of customer services calls to ensure the right steps and scripts were followed;
- Reviewing a sample of customer onboarding records to ensure they have all the right documentation attached;
- Reviewing a sample of underwriting data to ensure the right credit decision-making took place;
- Reviewing a sample of code being promoted to production to ensure it has all the correct checks and commentary and has been tested and evidenced; and
- Reviewing outbound customer communications to ensure compliance.

Not all assurance controls are created equal, and it's important that they are well designed. If not, they can result in wasted time as best, and missed issues at worst. In his book, *Risk Management Simplified,* Andy Osborne specifies six questions that risk management monitoring should answer in relation to the assurance controls put in place:

- Is it doing the job it's intended to do?
- Is it reducing overall exposure to risk?
- Does it improve efficiency?
- Does it continue to be cost effective?
- Is the level of residual risk acceptable?
- Is it being adhered to?[100]

This is a great list because, often, assurance just focuses on the final question about whether the control is being executed as planned, not whether it's a good or useful control. As the organisation matures, it should continually review its assurance practices for cost-benefit and efficiency and look to innovative ways to achieve the same ends. For example, all major banks are undergoing digitisation journeys right now – this poses a real opportunity to build in quality assurance and reporting, embedded within modern technology, rather than having old-school, after-the-fact inspections.

## Embedding alerts for risk issues

What sources are the committee and management getting their intel from? How are they being alerted when risk events take place? Ideally, a well-designed system of automated notifications and relevant metrics should tell them, in a timely manner, when things are going wrong.

For each key risk, the organisation should have set a risk tolerance and specified the operational risk indicators (ORIs), or triggers, that will show whether that risk is drifting out of tolerance. Monitoring these indicators and discussing them at the risk committee is an important measure for management to demonstrate that it is keeping within the guidelines. The more system-driven these can be, the more effective and efficient the monitoring. Automated monitoring means you can cover a large amount of ground, confident in the knowledge that the systems will alert you to breaches. When combined with anecdotal, people-based evidence as to what's happening on the ground (e.g. customer feedback, ratings, staff feedback), you have a strong combination of measures to watch.

As an example, one key weapon in the battle against fraud is transaction monitoring. This involves identifying the characteristics of behaviour (both customer and internal behaviour) that may be suspicious (e.g. employees emailing files to themselves, customers entering into unusual combinations of transactions) and highlighting those for further scrutiny. Given the volume and scale that organisations operate at, it's obvious how essential automated alerts are to support this process.

Finally, although automated monitoring is a powerful tool, don't forget the value of human judgement. Board members should have access to customers and staff, and vice versa, to hear anecdotal evidence about what is improving or disimproving. Finally, whistleblowing can be a valuable source of information for untoward behaviour. A whistleblowing hotline can be offered independently to the organisation, and it makes sense to have an independent person, at board level, to whom concerns are escalated.

## Summary

Governance can appear a dry topic, but failures of governance are anything but. When responsibilities are clear and when the board, committees, management and staff know what they need to do, and discharge those responsibilities accordingly, with transparent reporting and escalation, risk management can run smoothly. Governance is there to ensure these things happen. Ultimate responsibility for governance sits with the board, which makes those positions, and the actions of the people who occupy them, very important indeed.

# Chapter 14

## *Risk systems and models*

As we've seen in Chapter 8, technology is absolutely fundamental to the way we work. Our organisations and business models are becoming more complex and digitised over time. For the risk function to keep pace, it needs to be data-enabled, smart and efficient too. You have to fight fire with fire!

There are a wealth of technology solutions and data-modelling options available to the CRO. One obvious route is a risk management information system which aggregates risk data and supports evaluation of business risks. This poses significant advantages compared to the multiple databases and spreadsheets that organisations previously relied on, as it allows for a truly integrated system and understanding of what's occurring across departments and even different organisations.

As Russell Reynolds says, *"Building data and digital fluency in risk"* is a critical competency for CROs of the future, including *"understanding the potential benefits of technology adoption, and how data analytics can develop sophisticated models, predictive tools and greater understanding of trends."*[101]

# Integrated risk management systems

Smaller enterprises may well be able to manage their risk registers on spreadsheets. Once an organisation reaches a certain size and complexity, the benefits of an integrated risk management system become harder to refute, even if just to manage suppliers. A number of platforms lead with their third-party risk management software, recognising the administration overhead involved in onboarding and tracking suppliers, plus all their associated documents.

However, as with all software, the CRO should not expect a digital solution to be a panacea. A well-designed set of key risks, with risk events tracked against them, can be done on a spreadsheet, as can RCSAs. If risks, risk events and RCSAs are all a jumbled, incoherent mess, this needs to be resolved before you go down the software route. Be careful not to look to an information system alone to fix the problem, as the answers will only be as good as the data you feed into it. Start with clarity of vision, clear out the dead wood and get back to basics. Then, if the operational benefits of a software solution still look attractive, you can proceed with building or buying the platform you need.

Several organisations are working to digitise their risk management frameworks. They are doing this by codifying risks and controls, making them comparable across organisations and using consolidated data to help organisations benchmark themselves against their peers, identify gaps and find ways to strengthen their controls. Whether you choose a third-party solution or manage this in-house, it certainly helps to have a single, definitive set of key risks, a way of tracking risk events and control deficiencies against these as well as reports that track progress over time.

There is a growing and increasingly crowded marketplace for operational risk management system solutions. Some of the most popular solutions at time of writing include Acin, SAI Global, SureCloud, Riskconnect, RSA, OneTrust and IBM.[102]

Other common uses of information systems in risk include:

- **Portfolio management.** Digitising data allows for analysis of the composition of credit portfolios as well as identification of trends, performance, concentration, etc.
- **Assurance.** This involves using technology to check whether the defined policies and rules are being implemented correctly, for example in relation to customer onboarding and credit underwriting decisions. Automated checks will provide you with greater coverage and consistency than human checks ever could.

When choosing a risk management system, it's worth bearing in mind the following requirements:

*Functional requirements of risk systems*
- Provides standardised risk definitions and templates (think carefully about how much you customise these to your needs – one of the benefits of these systems is the ability to compare yourself to others);
- Allows for qualitative and quantitative descriptions of risk appetite (not just financial);
- Easy to capture risk event details, including root cause analysis;
- Ability to look at risks at varying levels of detail, to aggregate and disaggregate risks per department, area, region, etc.;
- Ability to capture and integrate business metrics and map to risk metrics (e.g. capturing number of business complaints and mapping to the conduct risk measure);
- Providing predictive analytics to anticipate where risks may occur;

- Intuitive reporting features, that express risk in terms business users will recognise and understand.

## Non-functional

- Intuitive user interface (easy for business teams to complete without tons of training);
- Cloud-based;
- Usable on desktops, mobiles etc.;
- Provides access to peer group information and benchmarking;
- Meets security and privacy requirements;
- Regularly updated to take account of changing regulation.

## Data and analytics

In our increasingly digitised world, data is power. Organisations are getting ever more sophisticated at understanding their customers, their behaviours and preferences. For a topical example, consider how smart meters were used to track the degree of adherence to Covid lockdown restrictions – whether or not you boil the kettle at home becomes a valuable insight when tracked and aggregated with the behaviour of millions of others.

As CRO, it's important to understand how your organisation is capturing, storing and using data. Some key questions to ask include:

- What data are we capturing, from whom and in what way?
- How are we using data to inform decisions (ensuring, of course, that it's ethical and legal)?
- How are we gathering this data (including the necessary disclosures and consents from the customer)?
- How confident are we that this data is a reliable predictor of the behaviours we expect (e.g. is the population representative? Is the chain of causation established)?

- How long are we holding the data for?
- Do we dispose of the data when no longer needed?

## Artificial intelligence and machine learning

Now we've captured the data, how do we put it to good use? How do we leverage this information to improve our business outcomes? Used in the right way, it can improve decision-making at scale in order to boost efficiency and drive down the cost-income ratio.

Artificial intelligence and machine learning, some of the most advanced technologies available, allow us to do this by applying algorithms and automating data modelling, enabling us to analyse trends and make robust predictions. It's like having an expert data scientist in-house who is able to harness the power of big data for the purposes of optimising your business. One of the positive advances in recent years is the democratisation of these services – open banking and technology enhancements now mean that services and models that help with everything from anti-money laundering, fraud prevention, credit prediction and vulnerability detection are increasingly widely available and relatively straightforward to deploy.

To better understand this area of growth, here are some quick and concise definitions of the key concepts:

- **A model.** Uses past inputs and outputs to predict a future outcome.
- **Artificial intelligence (AI).** The use of computing power to mimic human intelligence through the use of if-then logic, decision trees or machine learning.
- **Machine learning (ML).** A subset of AI which uses intelligence such that the model improves, or learns, over time.

- **Deep learning.** This is the most advanced form of ML, in which neural networks are exposed to huge amounts of data to allow machines to achieve complex functions such as voice recognition.

The widespread availability of algorithms, cheap computing and storage power have made the use of artificial intelligence and machine learning ever more prevalent in today's society. When you combine this availability with the business imperatives to reduce costs and boost efficiency, it's no surprise that organisations are looking to these models to improve decision-making at scale. As an example, here are some of the applications of big data in financial services:

- For credit decisioning, predicting the probability of default of a customer, based on certain variables. Data analysis can be used to justify a yes or no decision or to decide the price of credit to be offered;
- To predict the level of default in an overall loan portfolio;
- In debt collection, to engage customers in conversations when they fall overdue in their repayments. See, for example, how software from organisations such as Webio use ML to engage in a "dialogue" with customers, over chat, to help guide them through what would otherwise be a 40-minute collections conversation.

## Building a robust data model for decision-making

If your organisation is using, or intending to use, financial models, you need to consider the model strategy, the quality of the data inputs, how roles and responsibilities are assigned, mitigate any risk of discrimination or bias, manage the model through the life cycle, and consider appropriate oversight and governance.

*Model strategy*

When setting out to use a model to automate decision-making, it's important to understand the underlying rationale. Useful questions include:

- What is your model going to be used for? What is the business need? Is a model appropriate for this purpose?
- Is the model the primary decision-making factor? Will you use a secondary model or method alongside it?
- How much human interaction do you envisage?
- What is the business impact of less-than-perfect prediction by the model?
- What are the mitigants if that happens? For example, you might run an alternative model, do a sense-check alongside, or have humans check a sample of the results, as well as looking for overall trends.
- What oversight will you have in place?
- When will you kick out the automated results for human review?

Remember as well that, under GDPR, a customer has a right to have their case reviewed by a person, which means you need a backup method of assessment for, say, their credit application.

*Quality of data*

Regardless of the sophistication of the modelling techniques being used, one thing still holds true – the model is only as good as the data being used to train it. Therefore, as CRO, you should pay attention to where your organisation is sourcing the data from to train and validate the model. If garbage goes in, garbage comes out. The organisation needs to be asking:

- What is the source of our data inputs?
- How sure are we about the quality?

- How often is the data updated?
- Are there gaps in the data or duplicates?

If the population you are using to train your model does not reflect your current and future population, then you need to be prepared for the results to be suboptimal at best. So, if you train your credit model based on one subset of society, but you then lend to another, the results may not stand up. As the Russell Reynolds article says, CROs should *"commit to looking beyond 'impressive' models and dig into where the data has been sourced: take nothing for granted."*[103]

*Roles and responsibilities*

When devising a model, it's important to understand the distinct roles that different actors play across the three lines of defence.

First-line roles have primary responsibility within the business line, and key roles are:

- The **model owner**, who has overall responsibility for the business purpose and use of the model.
- The **model developer**, who creates the model in line with requirements and good practice.
- The **model user,** who will apply the model in a business capacity day-to-day.
- Second-line roles:
- The **model controller** is an independent second-line expert who provides challenge and oversight to the development, implementation and ongoing use of the model.
- Third-line roles:
- The **model reviewer** provides specialist and independent validation of the performance of the model. This can either be in advance of launching the model, or periodically, after it has been built, to ensure ongoing satisfactory performance.

*Discrimination and bias*

A model needs to be sufficiently discriminating to tell you the difference between a yes and a no (or whatever outcome you are modelling for). Its predictive quality is often measured using something called a Gini score.

However, there is also the risk that your model discriminates unfairly, particularly against protected characteristics such as gender, race, sexual orientation, etc. This is a complex and nuanced area. For example, car insurance companies typically charge women less as we are "better drivers". Is that fair? The data says yes – statistically, women are involved in fewer accidents. Will these practices continue to be acceptable to society? Time will tell. Being transparent about which characteristics the model uses is extremely important.

*Model life cycle*

Once the strategy, purpose and inputs of the model are clear, the model then moves through several stages of development during which the risk team can provide input.

- **Development**. What algorithmic model will be used? Will it be an open-source model (there are many of these widely available), or built in-house and bespoke? Will it use logistical regression, ML or other approaches? What are the assumptions, risks, issues and sensitivities behind its use?
- **Data**. What data will be used to train the model? Where will it be sourced?
- **Model testing**. This involves using a portion of the data that has not been used for training the model. Is the model sufficiently accurate and predictive without "over-fitting"? Do you need all the variables you are using, or would a

smaller set be almost as effective? Are you only gathering the data you need to inform decision-making?

- **Model implementation**. This includes embedding it in the organisation's workflow and existing systems. Don't neglect end-to-end testing at this point – the model will only be useful if it works alongside existing technology and processes.
- **Ongoing review and retraining**. Models deteriorate over time. They must be periodically retrained with newer data to ensure they remain effective.

*Governance and oversight*

When setting out the model framework, you must consider how it will be overseen, to ensure that it is used effectively and as intended, and where you will source the necessary skills from. Questions to ask include:

- Who approves the model for first use?
- Who tracks its performance?
- Who sets the limits for how much the model can be used, and how much risk exposure it will cover?

Also bear in mind that the use of AI / ML brings a whole new set of ethical and risk considerations that will need managing. How far the organisation goes in its use of these tools and managing the potential for detrimental outcomes will require close and ongoing scrutiny.

*Retraining and recalibration*

However good your model is on day one, it must be subject to regular review, retraining with fresh data and/or recalibration.

- Retraining is using a fresh or more up-to-date set of data and outcomes to retrain the model.

- Recalibration is still using the model logic as is, but moving the goalposts or changing the tolerances of the output of the model.

## Summary

Technology solutions for CROs are evolving all the time, as are data-modelling options. The key is to have a strong underlying rationale for their use, not to be dazzled by their complexity and to follow good practice around governance, oversight, development and monitoring. The technology may well be complex, but the underlying principles of good risk management stay the same.

# SECTION THREE - PULLING IT ALL TOGETHER

# Chapter 15

*Your risk team*

To build and maintain the risk infrastructure described in the preceding chapters, you are going to need a team around you, unless you're in a very small organisation. You need to consider how big a team you need, its composition and its traits and competencies. If you've inherited a team, you'll want to assess the skill sets that you have already, whether you have the balance you need and any changes you want to make.

Russell Reynolds also reminds us that "*developing bench strength for the risk function of the future*" is critical and includes "*rewarding, retaining, training and cross-training internal successors, as well as continuously infusing fresh outside talent*".[104]

Below I outline the key considerations for creating, maintaining and growing an effective risk team that will support your strategic aims.

## Size and composition

How big a team do you need, and how specialised do they need to be? This depends on a number of variables, including:

- the size of the overall organisation;
- the number of departments, product lines and geographies the organisation has;
- the complexity of the products;
- the degree of regulation your industry is subject to;
- how well-established the first line of defence is and how accepting of their role they are as 'owners' of their risk areas; and
- the risk-awareness and risk appetite of the executive team and board.

It must also be remembered that the bulk of risk management activity is the responsibility of the first line of defence – management. Therefore, staff in engineering, product and operations, simply by doing a good job and running a tight ship, are managing risk daily, and that's how it should be. You should not therefore calculate the size and makeup of your team on the basis they will singlehandedly shoulder the responsibility for risk in the organisation. They are there to support and guide the first line.

## Traits

In Chapter 2, we discussed the personality traits of the CRO. You would ideally like your team to both mirror and complement these traits. Your people need to be commercial, solutions-focused, analytical and relationship-focused. They should be able to stand back and see what the real risk is. They need to have the judgement and tenacity to ensure they are not being bogged down by the risk framework. They should be able to hold firm against the first line, but constructively so.

## Competencies

Useful competencies your team should have (or which you may need to insource) include the following:

- Business analysis / process mapping: the ability to understand and map what is actually going on within a department, and between departments. Where is the flow of money, of information; where do the handoffs take place, where are the weaknesses? This business analysis capability should be a core strength of a good proportion of your team.
- Data analytics and modelling: as we've seen, the use of data is gaining significance everywhere; some of your people need to be able to crunch data themselves, and also to advise business and tech users on good practice in in this space.
- Information and cybersecurity: this is an evolving and complex area. You need access to cyber professionals with up-to-the-minute knowledge, and the ability to deploy the right frameworks to identify vulnerabilities and prioritise remediation.
- Business continuity and resilience: an area that is changing rapidly in response to cloud adoption and the pandemic. The days of hot sites, cold sites and alternative working space may be somewhat behind us, but they have been replaced with a need for remote working solutions and operational resilience, so that organisations are less vulnerable to shocks. You will need a proportion of this capability in your team, or you'll need to outsource it.
- Project and programme management: finally, a much-overlooked skill – the ability to structure improvement plans, assign priorities, timelines, track progress and communicate clearly with stakeholders. Everyone can benefit from at least the rudiments of good programme delivery skills.

In addition, if your team members have had relevant first-line business experience and/or product specialism, that can be a great source of skills and understanding for a risk role. Having a balance within your team of "poachers and gamekeepers" is a great way of ensuring that relevance and realism balance out risk theory. Be open to the possibility of attracting people from the first line of defence into risk. There is no better risk professional than the one who has been on the front line, seen all the tricks of the trade and knows where the skeletons are buried.

## Hiring and developing talent

As a leader, it's important to build bench strength in your team. Even in the early days, you should think about talent development, progression and, ultimately, succession planning for your role. Don't fear those people who have ambition and who, ultimately, one day, would like to have your job.

An organisation ultimately gets the risk talent that it deserves. If it only pays lip service to risk management, deprioritises it and rolls over on the tough decisions, it should not expect to recruit and retain strong, capable and dynamic risk professionals – they simply won't stay. The ultimate attraction and retention tools for building a risk team (aside from salary etc.) are your leadership and the culture of the organisation, in particular its attitude to risk.

## Training

A robust, holistic development plan for your people ensures they continue to grow and adds more value to you and to the organisation. Taking the broadest view of development will ensure a blended and cost-effective learning experience. For example:

- A large proportion of training can be done "on the job" i.e. learning by doing. If internal skills are lacking and you opt to bring in some consultancy (e.g. to create a risk framework, business continuity plan or information security assessment), ensure you get an internal member of staff to partner with the consultant so the learning is brought in-house.
- A number of external accreditations are available, as shown in Chapter 2. These can be a significant investment of both time and money. Modularised courses allow for the work and the cost to be tailored to the need.
- Organisations, such as the Institute of Risk Management (www.theirm.org), offer members access to online resources, webinars, tools and techniques and help keep staff up to date on emerging topics.
- Publications such as www.risk.net will help the team keep abreast of risk topics in the financial services industry.

## Diversity

The biggest risk failures almost always cite contributing factors such as groupthink or a lack of imagination, foresight or bravery to call out things that were wrong or could go wrong. Too often, with hindsight, people say that they knew something was a potential problem. They may have tried to raise it and it was played down or suppressed, or there may have been so many issues that this was just one of many that got lost in the mix. Diversity in thinking reduces the risk of groupthink or complacency. Ensuring diversity in hiring practices is one solution to this underlying problem.

It has been proven, time and again, that people of different backgrounds, beliefs and experiences bring a more rounded view and are less complacent. Diversity is not just a nicety of the modern age; it is a tool that will improve how your organisation functions. However, beware an overbearing person in power, either within the risk team or outside, who seeks to suppress risks when they *are* raised. Dissenting voices from a diverse team are only useful if they are listened to.

You also want to balance diversity of skills and talent. For example, do you have sufficient digital-savvy staff to meet the challenges of digitisation, AI and cyber, alongside traditional risk expertise?

## Summary

Ultimately, the role of a leader is to leave things better than they found them. If you can attract, develop and retain a diverse body of strong, motivated and skilled risk professionals, you will have done your organisation a lasting service.

# Chapter 16

*Achieving the promise of great risk management*

So far, we have focused somewhat on the mechanics of risk management. This is essential when getting to grips with the role of CRO and when establishing, or assessing, a risk management framework.

However, this book is not just about how to create and implement a risk management framework. This is about how to be a great Chief Risk Officer. Risk management has been around now for 20 years. We have reams of frameworks and controls at our disposal. Entire libraries of reference material from which to draw. However, we're still a long way from the risk role achieving its full potential. I believe that, too often, risk is viewed as an impediment to the organisation and its progress. Frequently, organisations operate with a sense of resistance to risk management, adopting a "we'll have to get this past risk" attitude. This is partly because other teams do not fully understand the potential of the risk role in supporting the organisation and partly because risk professionals themselves, as I mentioned earlier in the book, do not always focus on actionable solutions.

I want to pose an alternative viewpoint and put forward the concept of the risk function as an *enabler* in the organisation. To be a great CRO, you need to be able to move beyond the risk management process towards a more active and creative role in the organisation, using your insight to drive progress forwards rather than holding it back. Below I've outlined five areas in which this leap needs to be made.

Risk professionals should strive to move from:

- Frameworks to judgement;
- Controls to empowerment;
- Risk-focus to a solutions-focus;
- Single risk factors to multi-layer insights; and
- Governance to action.

## From frameworks to judgement

The outcome of great risk management is not a PowerPoint presentation or an argument "won" – it's actionable insights which empower and enable management to do the right things. To achieve the organisation's outcomes at a manageable and calculable level of risk.

Too often, the presentation of the risk framework to the executive committee or board seems to be the endgame. The risk team presents the key risks, updates on the RCSAs and action plans on a quarterly basis. This is understandable given the considerable work required just to pull these things together to the requisite standard. However, unless you go further and provide your judgement, the organisation is missing out on the expert insight that all that work enables. The framework and its findings are the beginning of the conversation and not the end.

A great CRO will be able to digest and assimilate this content and ask the most pertinent questions, such as:

- Does the combination of the systems weakness in operations, the staff shortage and the audit findings on processes mean that we have a compounded risk in this area?

Or:

- The RCSA for technology suggests that our quality assurance (QA) framework is designed and operating effectively, yet 25% of the risk events we've had in the past quarter relate to testing failures. Can these two things be true?
- Or, ultimately:
- Are we doing OK? Or are there risks in plain sight that we've become complacent about?

This application and interrogation of the facts is where the true value of the CRO lies.

## Moving from controls to empowerment

Rather than saying, "We could lose £Xm on this venture" and being paralysed by the prospect, the CRO can turn this around and focus on what *is* possible within acceptable risk parameters instead of shutting down progress. Try to outline what positive action they can take: "With the measures we have in place, management is empowered to risk up to £1m on this venture. As long as the organisation is learning and we continue to believe in this prospect, keep us posted on progress, and come back when you're nearing that threshold."

The process of explicitly prioritising risks according to severity and financial impact and getting collective ExCo agreement on what they will, and will not, worry about demonstrates that you are being measured in your investment and accepting the smaller risks that fall below the line.

Of course, there are different considerations when concepts such as ethics and reputation come into play, as a small incident can have a disproportionate impact on brand perception. These therefore require a slightly different approach. Here, I strongly recommend the organisation works on a sense of values, behaviours and principles. In other words, culture. However, in the main, offering your organisation the concept of "freedom within a framework" is good practice and empowering.

## From a risk-focus to a solutions-focus

Too often, risk professionals can fall into the trap of pointing out all the potential pitfalls of a venture and walk away with a sense of a job well done. In this case, all you have done is slow down the organisation. Of course, there will be times (when a particular venture is ill-advised) that slowing down the organisation is a good thing. However, mostly it will be perceived as putting blockers in the way of the organisation's progress.

One organisation I worked with changed this risk-focus attitude simply by enacting a change of language. Instead of saying, "We can't, because …", they turned it around to, "We can, if …". This provides the CRO with a new, more challenging, but more value-adding position to take. It may be a subtle difference, but changing the language can significantly alter the effect it has on teams and the organisation as a whole. Here are some examples:

- "We can lend to this group of customers, as long as we satisfy ourselves on affordability."
- "We can launch in this new country, if we review the regulatory regime and limit our exposure to X."
- "We can launch this product, if we can demonstrate that it meets the user requirements and has less than X% errors."

This is harder to do than pointing out the problems, as it requires some more creative thinking to find the opportunity even when that opportunity is slim and difficult to exploit. It will make many risk professionals uncomfortable because you are getting off the fence and endorsing an approach. However, you will be a better partner to the organisation if you embrace the discomfort and attempt to offer positive solutions.

## From single risk factors to multi-layer insights

When discussing the risks the organisation faces, unless you consider the interplay between different risk factors, you are only getting a one-dimensional view. The real power comes when you start to join up the patterns and see risk holistically.

Take, for example, a situation where a cyber risk has been sitting on amber for a couple of quarters. Horizon scanning has shown an uptick in malicious attacks. A staffing gap due to a departure in the information security team has been unfilled. Plus, the company has just had quite a bit of publicity about a new product close to being launched. It doesn't take much to string these factors together and realise that the prospect of a ransomware attack is a good deal higher than management would probably like it to be. This level of insight is rare, and it takes a thoughtful CRO to draw them out and expose them to management. This is art as much as science, but this is what can make the ultimate difference.

## From governance to action

Finally, even if we provide our insights on the facts, it's critical that the risk role doesn't stop with reporting and governance. It's not enough to say, "Well, we've briefed the board on the risks, our job here is done." Again, we have to go further and ask, "What are we going to do about it?" We need to spur the organisation to action, rather than allow issues to build up over time without being resolved. This goes back to the importance of execution: a risk management framework is worthless if it is not being used on the ground.

Organisations everywhere have risk registers that show risks that are apparently outside of their risk appetite, and this can go on for months, quarters or even years. I believe it's time to end the complacency that comes with that. If risks are outside appetite, either the organisation is taking risks that it should not, or the organisation's risk appetite has been set too low. This is why I say that setting risk appetite is a non-trivial exercise. It's not enough to say, "We have a very low tolerance for loss." Well, of course you do! Everyone does. However, reducing risk to zero is unlikely and expensive. Fostering honest conversations about what the real appetite for risk is will help to clear out those cobwebbed, less critical risks that have been sitting around for too long, and instead focus the organisation on what is real and pressing.

There is a cost of implementing controls in an organisation, and these must be weighed up against the benefits (and, of course, against any legal or regulatory requirements). If risk appetite has been set thoughtfully and your organisation is genuinely outside of that, management needs to take action – now. Of course, it may be the case that management and the board actually have a higher risk appetite than they think. Perhaps up to £50 or even £50,000 of stock wastage every month is not that big a deal, especially if the solution to remove that problem costs a multiple of that.

CROs need to challenge management to calibrate risk appetite properly, to counter-propose the cost of mitigation measures and to have an intelligent conversation about options. If, after all that, the organisation is still operating outside their risk appetite, then it really should be doing something about it.

## Summary

The successful execution of all the technical aspects of risk management is table stakes for the CRO. Over and above excellent day-to-day management, information gathering, assessment and reporting, the CRO must never rest in keeping the organisation alert to the risks it's incurring. This involves seeing beyond the obvious, making connections, proposing solutions and taking action. This is what discerns good from great.

# Chapter 17

*Seeing the wood from the trees*

In his book, *Tame, Messy and Wicked Risk Leadership*, Dr David Hancock says: *"The more we stare at the jumble of equations and models, the more we lose sight of what risk is all about. Knowing how risk management works is just the beginning. Knowing how and when to use these tools is the art of risk management."* [105]

As we've seen in the previous chapter, seeing the wood from the trees is perhaps the greatest skill of a CRO – the art of applying their judgement and providing holistic insights. The senior role is as demanding as any at the C-suite level, and the work will expand to (more than) fit the space available. With your time at a premium, perhaps the greatest danger for a CRO is to become so consumed in the mechanics of the day-to-day role – the meetings, committees, RCSAs and audits – that they miss something. This might be a creeping risk that isn't addressed quickly enough or a complacent organisational culture that says, "Well, we always did it this way", or, "Everybody in the sector does the same". It might be a cultural shift that encourages your customers to decide that, no, they don't like how your organisation does things any more. Or it could just be a gradual deterioration in a combination of risk controls you are using which, on their own, look innocent enough, but when added together, create a critical weakness.

It's difficult to do, but you simply must carve out enough time periodically to stand back and reflect on the bigger picture and do some blue-sky thinking. There are some risks that may be lurking in plain sight and which may only require a small shift in perspective to bring them into full focus.

## Scanning for black swans

In spite of all our preparations, occasionally a risk emerges that we are not prepared for, almost out of nowhere. In financial services, these are referred to as "black swans".

Covid is a perfect example of this – an extremely rare event with extreme consequences that changed the context entirely. Was Covid a black swan? Well, yes and no. For years, epidemiologists had talked about the prospect of a bat-related virus. Climate experts had warned that if we continued to mess with climate and biodiversity and drive animals from their natural habitats, that could give rise to new variants. Geopolitical instability means that countries continue to research and develop bioweapons. Hollywood even produced the movie *Contagion*. So, technically, the risk was always there and known about.

Most business continuity plans made provision for some kind of pandemic. However, we perhaps envisaged a short period of time when staff were unavailable to work because they were unwell. So, we perhaps made staffing backup plans, looked at key man risk and so on. We didn't, however, envisage a scenario when our staff could (largely) keep working but when entire cities became redundant for a period of over a year. Large organisations with older technology and "only 2,000 VPN lines" to dial into the office never imagined 100% of staff working remotely. Credit analysts have had to deal with a whole new set of scenarios – are parts of the economy dead or merely in frozen animation, waiting to reawaken when the virus passes?

In August 2020, Acin and Fitch[106] partnered on research which showed the impact of Covid on:

- People and increased conduct risk;
- Processes, including making offices Covid-ready with deep cleaning etc., but also supervision and coaching; and
- IT and systems, including the increased need for home working and cloud-based platforms.

Risk teams would do well to re-examine their key risks in the light of this new environment we are living in. They may find that risk appetite has changed, as has the profile of some of their most critical risks. The global pandemic has changed our lives more than anything since the world wars – our risk frameworks will need to adapt too.

## Emerging topics

The context within which we work changes quickly and constantly. It pays to track trends and search for emerging topics which could have an impact on your organisation and thus your risk framework. Below are a number of changes that are particularly topical at the time of writing:

- **New industries of systemic importance.** Not so long ago, if you asked people to list areas of the economy that were of systemic importance, you would have thought about utilities and banks. We probably didn't consider supermarkets and pharmaceutical companies as integral. During the pandemic and its aftermath, we patiently queued outside supermarkets and we now think about the fragility of our food chain. Even a temporary glitch in the vaccine supply chain has political repercussions and social and economic implications. As these industries grow in prominence and importance, they also need to be resilient to shocks in order to ensure continuity of service and supply.

- **Operational resilience**. Even before the pandemic, regulators, particularly in financial services, were moving beyond the concepts of business continuity and business resumption planning and towards the direction of building resilience. This means designing processes and systems to be strong enough to prevent interruptions or withstand and bypass them when they occur. It's an emerging topic which has been propelled forward by Covid. There is more work to be done by all in this area, although it must be said that many organisations coped admirably with the disruption caused by Covid as they trusted their staff to be innovative and adaptable.

- **Distributed operations.** The pandemic will likely leave us with a workforce that is, and wants to be, more widely distributed geographically. Zoom and Teams calls will be a part of our future, no matter what. What does this mean for monitoring and supervision? How can you assure that procedures are being followed? What does it mean for the training and mentoring of staff? Again, we must evolve and adapt to this new context but also consider the risks and manage them effectively.

- **Climate risk**. There were some who thought that our preoccupation with Covid would mean that the focus on climate and loss of biodiversity would wane. In fact, it appears that the opposite is the case. People seem more keenly aware of nature, our abuse of it and the implications of this abuse than ever before. As ever, younger people are at the forefront of the movement. However, even the mainstream, including regulators and investors, are taking notice of the climate threat and want organisations to explain their role.

- **Cost optimisation**. The financial cost of the pandemic, in terms of lost productivity, healthcare and all those long months of economic support, is on a scale not seen since wartime. My belief is that we will need some kind of global "new deal" to reset the world economy. There are economic inflationary measures that will help us to somewhat outgrow the debts that have been incurred, but there is no escaping the vast economic cost. How will this play out for organisations? Are we entering a period of austerity or something else?

- **Deepfake threats and loss of trust**. Perhaps it was only a matter of time before our technology was harnessed for such ill means, but the rise of "alternative facts" and the emergence of deepfake technology will only further erode trust in future years. What do you do when you can't be sure a person is really saying what they appear to be saying on TV or online? How will media organisations retain or regain trust? Will pernicious vested interests be exposed? This will require concerted effort and skill.

- **The role of technology platforms**. At the time of writing, many organisations have made the move, quite happily, to the use of cloud technology. The benefits it offers vs. on-site storage are many: reduced cost and technology headcount, flexibility, redundancy, the ability to spin up new instances and not having to worry about infrastructure upgrades. Some organisations will still hold back because of concerns, primarily about privacy – how can their customers' data be guaranteed to be secure? – and systemic risk i.e. losing the data altogether, or access to it. If all the large organisations of the world are housing their tech on the platforms of Amazon, Microsoft and a few others, we have a whole new area of systemic risk – the security and availability of cloud infrastructure – to think about. My view is that these probably do a far better job than small, individual technology departments could do in the past. Plus, their multi-location strategy, with real-time resilience and failover, mitigate much of the risk. However, perhaps more needs to be done by the technology and risk community to discuss this topic and reassure and explain to stakeholders why they can reasonably make the leap.

- **Geopolitical risk**. Finally, it feels as if we live in a time of increased geopolitical risk. Whether it's Brexit, the war in Ukraine or a tumultuous few years in the US, Russia and Brazil, it feels like one of those times when the political tectonic plates are shifting and tremors are being felt everywhere. Whether we move forwards or backwards, together or apart, remains to be seen.

## Summary

Risk management as a profession doesn't always have a shiny image. For some, it conjures up notions of clipboards, naysayers and bureaucrats. As a risk professional, I have to admit that we have not always covered ourselves in glory. It can be very easy to fall into the trap of just pointing out pitfalls and reasons why things cannot be done – there are so many ways that things *can* go wrong! However, we are doing ourselves and our organisations and industries a disservice if that's all we do.

Instead, when we partner and bend our minds to how things *can* be done, in a safe and well-managed way, we advance the course of innovation, we empower our progressive minds and we drive human capability forward. Then, from that place of collaboration, when we really do have to get our colleagues to see and accept the exposures and risks we highlight, it's done from a place of partnership and trust.

Risk management matters. Lives and livelihoods depend on it. When pension schemes collapse, people who have worked all their lives suffer terribly in their old age. When financial products are mis-sold, people lose their homes, their peace of mind and their dignity. When a financial product, a drug or even an online game don't meet with expectations, trust is eroded and brands and organisations are damaged. People suffer injuries, illness or worse.

Make no mistake, good risk management is a noble cause. It makes lives better. It instils trust. It prevents damage and injury. It is not an easy role, but few things that are valuable are easy.

I wish you well in your risk management career and your path, hopefully, to Chief Risk Officer. I hope that this book has helped you on the way.

# Appendix

In this Appendix, I've collated a list of useful reference materials that should support you in your role as CRO.

- A list of policies and procedures;
- A list of key risks; and
- Sample operational risk indicators.

## List of policies and procedures

Legal and compliance:

- Whistleblowing;
- Anti-bribery and corruption;
- Anti-slavery;
- Anti-money laundering;
- Financial promotions (if applicable);
- Data protection;
- Data breach policy;
- Subject access rights process;
- Confidentiality;
- Conflicts of interest; and
- Record retention.

Sales and marketing:

- Social media policy.

Human Resources:

- Disciplinary policy;
- Staff development;
- Employee handbook;
- Holiday;
- Expenses;
- Redundancy and redeployment; and
- Home working.

Risk:

- Risk management framework;
- Business continuity plan;
- Fraud risk management;
- New product approval; and
- Risk and control self-assessment.

Operations:

- Third-party/outsourcing/supplier management.

Credit risk:

- Collections and recoveries;
- Creditworthiness and affordability; and
- Financing and credit risk policy.

Customer services:

- Vulnerable customers; and
- Complaints.

Engineering:

- Bring your own device;
- Systems access;
- Acceptable use;
- Incident management; and
- Change management.

# List of key risks

| Type of risk | Key risks | Risk description |
|---|---|---|
| Financial | Capital and liquidity | Risk that the organisation does not have adequate financial resources to meet its debts as they fall due. |
| Operational | Change management | Risk that the organisation fails to respond to change or fails to execute needed changes in the organisation. |
| People | Conduct | Risk that the behaviour of people within the organisation leads to adverse customer consequences. |
| Financial | Credit and counterparty | Risk that customers or counterparties do not pay the organisation what they owe, or that the portfolio does not operate in line with expectations. |
| Technology | Cyber or information security | Risk that the confidentiality, integrity or availability of the organisation's data is harmed. |
| Technical | Data privacy | Risk of the organisation's sensitive data being breached, leaked or shared. |
| Operational | Financial crime | Risk that the organisation is involved in money laundering, terrorist financing, bribery and corruption or sanctions breaches. |

| Type of risk | Key risks | Risk description |
|---|---|---|
| Financial | Financial reporting | Risk that the organisation's financial or tax situation is misstated, or that the organisation fails to file timely and accurate accounts. |
| Operational | Fraud | Risk that the organisation is a victim of internal or external fraudulent activities. |
| Technical | IT and platform | Risks to the availability or reliability of the organisation's technical platform. |
| Operational | Legal | Risk that the organisation fails to comply with the law or mismanages legal disputes. |
| Financial | Market | Risk that the financial markets move adversely to the organisation's interests. |
| Operational | Model | Risk that data models used by the organisation fail to perform as expected, resulting in outcomes that are different to those expected. |

| Type of risk | Key risks | Risk description |
|---|---|---|
| People | People | Risk that the organisation is unable to source the talent it requires in the right place or at the right time and cost, or that the organisation fails to meet its obligations to its staff. Or risk that staff underperform or of grievances, capability issues, bullying, harassment or other employee relations issues. |
| Operational | Physical security | Risk that the organisation's premises are unavailable, breached or suffer damage. |
| Operational | Product | Risk that the organisation's products do not meet customer expectations. |
| Operational | Regulatory | Risk that the organisation fails to meet its regulatory requirements. |
| Strategic | Strategic | Risk that the organisation fails to stay relevant in its market, fails to adopt to market changes or makes the wrong decisions regarding prioritisation, market or channel selection, or M&A activity. |
| Operational | Supplier or third party | Risk that the organisation's suppliers fail to meet their obligations. |
| Operational | Transaction processing | Risk of errors in the organisation's core processing activities. |

# Sample operational risk indicators

| Principal risk | Sample risk indicator |
| --- | --- |
| IT and platform | No. of incidents (P1, P2, P3 etc.). SLA breaches. |
| Data privacy | No. of data privacy incidents. No. of data subject access requests (SARs). Volume of customers or customer attributes being processed. |
| Cyber and information security | Successful cyberattacks. Cyberattack near misses. |
| Supplier and third party | No. of suppliers (Tier 1, 2, 3) missing SLAs. Third-party due diligence checks in time. Third parties with assigned owners, up-to-date meetings, contract in term, etc. |
| Change management | No. of new product approvals (NPAs) in progress, rejected or disputed etc. |
| Credit and counterparty | Single loss events. Number and value of credit write offs vs. policy. Portfolio concentration. Financial loss ratio in excess of policy. No. of loans in forbearance (if applicable). |

| Principal risk | Sample risk indicator |
|---|---|
| People and HR | No. of vacancies open.<br>Sickness or absence in excess of norms.<br>Staff turnover.<br>Misconduct and disciplinaries.<br>Staff morale and engagement indicators (e.g. internal NPS using a system like Officevibe).<br>External indicators e.g. Glassdoor. |
| Product | Net Promoter Score (NPS)<br>No. of complaints.<br>Satisfaction ratings.<br>Customer feedback ratings.<br>Customer lifetime value to customer acquisition cost (LTV/CAC).<br>No. of active customers vs. plan (WAU, DAU).<br>Customer "stickiness" measures.<br>External indicators e.g. App Store, Trustpilot. |
| Fraud | No. of internal and external fraud events or attempts.<br>Financial losses to fraud. |
| Financial crime | No. of suspicious activity reports (SARs) raised.<br>No. of sanctions breaches.<br>Customer exits and declines for financial crime reasons. |

| Principal risk | Sample risk indicator |
| --- | --- |
| Conduct | Customer satisfaction and chats rated "good" or above. Percentage of complaints resolved within SLA. |
| Transaction processing | Percentage of operational errors and manual corrections. |
| Regulatory | No. of reports to regulators. No. of regulatory breaches and SLA breaches. |
| Legal | No. of ongoing litigation cases. |
| Model | Measures of performance and outcome vs. model. |
| Capital and liquidity | Cash at bank vs. threshold level. Contingency funding. Months of spend left. |
| Market | Financial gains and losses. Hedging losses. Interest payments vs. model. Cost of funding vs. assumptions. |
| Financial reporting | No. of reporting errors. Audits past due. Auditor outstanding queries. |
| Physical security | No. of physical security incidents. Fire regulations last tested. Home-working proportion. BCP last tested. |
| Strategic | Market share. Sales trends. Share of customer wallet. New subscriptions. |

# Acknowledgements

My thanks to the technical reviewers and experts who generously gave of their time to provide input and feedback, including; Bronwyn Boyle, John Christiansen, Ian Ewart, Julien Haye, Cameron Holt, Anne Kiely, Ann Latham, Cormac O'Neill, Len Sinclair and Sarah Walsh.

Thank you to my editors, Sarah Busby and Andrew Dawson, for their flair and polish.

Particular thanks to Dr. Madhvi Vaghela for her contribution of the NHS case study on sustainability in chapter 11.

Thanks to my coach, Paula Boyle, who constantly challenges and inspires me.

Thanks to the Self-Publishing School, for helping with all the technical aspects of bringing this book into being.

Thank you to the following wonderful authors for contributing such strong content and for allowing me to reference their material where permission was required. Every effort has been made to trace the owners of copyright material. If there are any omissions, please contact jennifer@coo-author.com

Attenborough, D. *A Life on Our Planet: My Witness Statement and a Vision for the Future* (2020)

Chouinard, Y. & Stanley, V. *The Responsible Company: What We've Learned from Patagonia's First 40 Years* (2016)

Drysdale, A. *The Financial Controller: The Things the Academics Don't Teach You* (2010)

Hopkin, P. *Fundamentals of Risk Management: Understanding, Evaluating and Implementing Effective Risk Management* (2018)

Hillson, D. *The Risk Management Handbook: A Practical Guide to Managing the Multiple Dimensions of Risk* (2020)

Hancock, D. *Tame, Messy and Wicked Risk Leadership* (2010)

Lloyd, B. *Enterprise Risk Management* (2010)

McKeown, M. *The Strategy Book: How to Think and Act Strategically to Deliver Outstanding Results*, 3rd ed. (2019)

Osborne, A. *Risk Management Simplified: A practical, step-by-step guide to identifying and addressing risks to your business* (2010)

Rumelt, R. *Good Strategy/Bad Strategy: The Difference and Why it Matters* (2011)

Theobald, O. *Machine Learning for Absolute Beginners: A Plain English Introduction*, 3rd ed. (2021)

*Enterprise Risk* magazine, from the IRM. Available quarterly at www.enterpriseriskmag.com.

# References

## Chapter 1: The role of the Chief Risk Officer

1 Aksel, Kaan. "Organizing a Financial Institution to Deliver Enterprise-Wide Risk Management." PricewaterhouseCoopers. Accessed September 7, 2021. https://www.pwc.com.tr/en/assets/about/svcs/abas/frm/operationalrisk/articles/pwc_enterprisewiderisk.pdf

2 Yaffe, Ellen, Strong, Jake and Zhu, Beijing. "The Future of the Chief Risk Officer." Russell Reynolds Associates. September 10, 2020. Accessed September 7, 2021. https://www.russellreynolds.com/insights/thought-leadership/future-of-chief-risk-officer

3 Holberton, Dawn, McAndrew, Dougie and Simpson, Craig. "What Makes a Successful Risk Leader?" Risk Management Magazine. April 1, 2019. Accessed September 7, 2021. http://www.rmmagazine.com/2019/04/01/what-makes-a-successful-risk-leader/

4 Russell Reynolds Associates. "Where Do Chief Risk Officers Come From? Findings from an Analysis of CRO Career Paths at 50 of the World's Largest Banks." Russell Reynolds Associates. August 1, 2014. Accessed September 7, 2021. https://www.russellreynolds.com/insights/thought-leadership/where-do-chief-risk-officers-come-from

5 Ibid.

6 Enterprise Risk Magazine. "Women in Risk – Here Come The Girls!" Enterprise Risk Magazine. Accessed September 7, 2021. https://enterpriseriskmag.com/women-in-risk/

7 De Groot, Juliana. "Chief Risk Officer: What is a CRO? (and Why You Need One)"

https://digitalguardian.com/blog/chief-risk-officer-what-cro-and-why-you-need-one

8 Yaffe, Ellen, Strong, Jake and Zhu, Beijing. "The Future of the Chief Risk Officer."

9 Abrahams, Daniel. "A Journey from CRO to CEO." Bond University. Accessed September 7, 2021. https://bond.edu.au/intl/journey-cro-ceo

10 Hopkin, Paul. *Fundamentals of Risk Management: Understanding, Evaluating and Implementing Effective Risk Management, 5th edition.* London: Kogan Page Ltd, 2018.

11 Holberton, Dawn, McAndrew, Dougie and Simpson, Craig. "What Makes a
12 Goyder, Caroline. *Gravitas: Communicate with Confidence, Influence and Authority.* London: Vermilion, 2014.

12 Holberton, Dawn, McAndrew, Dougie and Simpson, Craig. "What Makes a Successful Risk Leader?"

14 Ibid.

## Chapter 2: The importance of a risk-aware culture

15 Hindson, Alex. "Risk Culture." In: Hillson, David ed. *The Risk Management Handbook.* London: Kogan Page, 2016.

16 Wint, S. "Guidance for Sound Practice." Enterprise Risk Magazine, Winter 2020. Accessed Jan 8, 2022.

17 Financial Stability Board. "Guidance on Supervisory Interaction with Financial Institutions on Risk Culture: A Framework for Assessing Risk Culture." Financial Stability Board. April 7, 2014. Accessed September 7, 2021. https://www.fsb.org/wp-content/uploads/140407.pdf

18 Adams, John, Anderson, Richard, Avery, Gill et al. "Risk Culture: Resources for Practitioners." The Institute of Risk Management. 2012. Accessed September 7, 2021. https://www.theirm.org/media/7230/risk-culture-resources-for-practitioners.pdf

19 Ibid.

20 Ibid.

21 DeLoach, Jim. "The Importance of Risk Culture." Corporate Compliance Insights. May 26, 2015. Accessed September 7, 2021. https://www.corporatecomplianceinsights.com/the-importance-of-risk-culture/#:~:text=Risk%20culture%20is%20the%20%E2%80%9Cset,all%20 organizations%2C%20whether%20public%20or

22 Adams, John, Anderson, Richard, Avery, Gill et al. "Risk Culture: Resources for Practitioners." The Institute of Risk Management. 2012. Accessed September 7, 2021. https://www.theirm.org/media/7230/risk-culture-resources-for-practitioners.pdf

23 Taylor, Larry. "Boards Should Monitor the Tone from the Bottom." NACD. Accessed Jan 8, 2022 https://www.nacdonline.org/insights/magazine/article. cfm?itemnumber=8894

24 Hunt, Jeremy. "From a blame culture to a learning culture." Department of Health and Social Care. March 10, 2016. Accessed September 7, 2021. https:// www.gov.uk/government/speeches/from-a-blame-culture-to-a-learning-culture

25 Meloni, G. "Ethics in Risk Management." In: Hillson, David. ed. *The Risk Management Handbook*. London: Kogan Page, 2016

26 Ripley, Mark. "The Orange Book: Management of Risk – Principles and Concepts." Government Finance Function. 2020. Accessed September 7, 2021. https://assets.publishing.service.gov.uk/government/uploads/system/ uploads/attachment_data/file/866117/6.6266_HMT_Orange_Book_Update_ v6_WEB.PDF

27 Ibid.

28 Schein, Edgar. *Organizational Culture and Leadership, 5th Edition*. Hoboken, New Jersey: John Wiley & Sons, 2017.

29 Ibid.

30 Project Management Institute. "PMI Ethical Decision-Making Framework (EDMF)." Project Management Institute. 2011. Accessed September 8, 2021. https://www.pmi.org/-/media/pmi/documents/public/pdf/ethics/ethical-decision-making-framework.pdf

31 https://goleansixsigma.com/dmaic-five-basic-phases-of-lean-six-sigma/

32 Adams, John, Anderson, Richard, Avery, Gill et al. "Risk Culture: Resources for Practitioners." The Institute of Risk Management. 2012. Accessed September 7, 2021. https://www.theirm.org/media/7230/risk-culture-resources-for-practitioners.pdf

## Chapter 3: Risk and organisational strategy: The foundation of your risk framework

33 International Organization for Standardization. "ISO 31000 – Risk Management." International Organization for Standardization. 2018. Accessed September 8, 2021. https://www.iso.org/publication/PUB100426.html

34 NHS Estates. "An exemplar operational risk management strategy." Department of Health. 1997. Accessed September 8, 2021. https://assets. publishing.service.gov.uk/government/uploads/system/uploads/attachment_ data/file/1009804/withdrawn_An_exemplar_operational_risk_management_ strategy.pdf

35 Ibid.

36 International Organization for Standardization. "ISO 31000 – Risk Management."

37 Ibid.

38 Hopkin, Paul. *Fundamentals of Risk Management.*

## Chapter 4: Risk and execution

39 https://twitter.com/elonmusk/status/1507777261654605828?lang=en Accessed 27 April, 2022.

40 Wint, S. "Guidance for Sound Practice." Enterprise Risk Magazine, Winter 2020. Accessed Jan 8, 2022.

41 Schreier, Jason. "Inside Cyberpunk 2077's Disastrous Rollout." Bloomberg. January 16, 2021. Accessed September 8, 2021. https://www.bloomberg.com/ news/articles/2021-01-16/cyberpunk-2077-what-caused-the-video-game-s-disastrous-rollout

42 Ibid.

**Chapter 5: The risk management process: Building your risk framework**

43   NHS Estates. "An exemplar operational risk management strategy." NHS Estates.

44 The Institute of Risk Management. "A Risk Management Standard." The Institute of Risk Management. 2002. Accessed January 26, 2022. https://www.theirm.org/media/4709/arms_2002_irm.pdf

45 Adams, John, Anderson, Richard, Avery, Gill et al. "Risk Culture: Resources for Practitioners." The Institute of Risk Management. 2012. Accessed September 7, 2021. https://www.theirm.org/media/7230/risk-culture-resources-for-practitioners.pdf

46 https://home.kpmg/be/en/home/insights/2020/10/blc-business-continuity-and-resilience.html  Accessed May 19, 2022

47   https://www.iso.org/standard/77008.html Accessed May 19, 2022.

**Chapter 6: Strategic risk**

**48**  Deloitte. "Exploring Strategic Risk: 300 executives around the world say their view of strategic risk is changing." Deloitte. 2013. Accessed September 8, 2021. https://www2.deloitte.com/content/dam/Deloitte/global/Documents/Governance-Risk-Compliance/dttl-grc-exploring-strategic-risk.pdf

49 Ibid.

50   http://www.businessdictionary.com/definition/strategic-risk.html Archived and now available at https://web.archive.org/web/20181219045008/http://www.businessdictionary.com/definition/strategic-risk.html

51 Kaplan, Robert and Mikes, Annette. "Managing Risks: A New Framework." Harvard Business Review. 2021. Accessed September 8, 2021. https://hbr.org/2012/06/managing-risks-a-new-framework

52 Ibid.

53 Deloitte. "Exploring Strategic Risk."

54  McKeown, Max. *The Strategy Book: How to think and act strategically to deliver outstanding results.* Third edition. Harlow: Pearson Education Ltd, 2020.

55 Rumelt, Richard. *Good Strategy/Bad Strategy: The Difference and Why it Matters.* London: Profile Books Ltd, 2012.

56  Hopkin, Paul. *Fundamentals of Risk Management.*


**Chapter 7: People risk**

57The Institute of Operational Risk. "People Risk Management – A Practical Approach to Managing the Human Factors That Could Harm Your Business." August 10, 2015. Accessed January 26, 2022. https://www.ior-institute.org/publications/people-risk-management-a-practical-approach-to-managing-the-human-factors-that-could-harm-your-business

58  KPMG. "Putting the framework together." KPMG. 2017. Accessed September 8, 2021. https://home.kpmg/content/dam/kpmg/uk/pdf/2017/09/conduct_risk_framework.pdf

59  Clark, Pilita. "Think that working from home is here to stay? Think again." The Irish Times. February 15, 2021. Accessed September 8, 2021. https://www.irishtimes.com/business/work/think-that-working-from-home-is-here-to-stay-think-again-1.4484553


**Chapter 8: Technology risk**

60  International Organization for Standardization. "ISO/IEC 27001 – Information Security Management." International Organization for Standardization. Accessed September 8, 2021. https://www.iso.org/isoiec-27001-information-security.html

61 COBIT. "COBIT: An ISACA Framework." ISACA. 2019. Accessed September 8, 2021. https://www.isaca.org/resources/cobit

62  Ibid.

63 National Institute of Standards and Technology. "NIST Cybersecurity Framework." National Institute of Standards and Technology. April 16, 2018. Accessed September 8, 2021. https://www.nist.gov/cyberframework

64   Ibid.

65https://gdpr.eu/eu-gdpr-personal-data/ Accessed May 27, 2022.

66 https://ico.org.uk/for-organisations/guide-to-data-protection/guide-to-the-general-data-protection-regulation-gdpr/accountability-and-governance/data-protection-impact-assessments/ Accessed May 27, 2022.

## Chapter 9: Financial risk

67   FCA sourcebook https://www.handbook.fca.org.uk/handbook/CONC/5/2A.html Accessed May 16, 2022.

68   Basel Committee on Banking Supervision. "Principles for the Management of Credit Risk." Bank for International Settlements. September 2000. Accessed May 16, 2022. https://www.bis.org/publ/bcbs75.pdf

69 Segal, Troy. "Five C's of Credit." Investopedia. August 25, 2021. Accessed September 8, 2021. https://www.investopedia.com/terms/f/five-c-credit.asp

70 https://www.fca.org.uk/publication/research/financial-lives-experiences-of-vulnerable-consumers.pdf Accessed May 16, 2022.

71   https://www.fca.org.uk/publication/research/vulnerability-exposed-research.pdf Accessed May 16, 2022.

72   Deloitte. "Reducing financial reporting risk." Deloitte. 2010. Accessed September 9, 2021. https://www.iasplus.com/en/binary/dttpubs/1002reducingrisk.pdf

## Chapter 10: Operational risk

73 Basel Committee on Banking Supervision. "Principles for the Sound Management of Operational Risk." Bank for International Settlements. June 2011. Accessed September 9, 2021. https://www.bis.org/publ/bcbs195.pdf

74 https://iasme.co.uk/counter-fraud-fundamentals

75 Deutsche Bank. "Operational Risk." Deutsche Bank. 2014. Accessed January 16, 2022. https://annualreport.deutsche-bank.com/2014/ar/management-report/risk-report/operational-risk.html

76 KPMG. "Banks' climate-related disclosures." Phase 1, April 2022.

## Chapter 11: Sustainability risk

77 Hindson, Alex; "What is the relevance of the rise of ESG to Chief Risk Officers?" Accessed May 17, 2022.https://www.riskcoalition.org.uk/blog-posts/what-is-the-relevance-of-the-rise-of-esg-to-chief-risk-officers-x765a

78 Our Common Future, The Brundtland Commission Report, 1987.

79 https://www.ferma.eu/what-do-we-mean-by-sustainability-and-sustainability-risks/ Accessed May 18, 2022.

80 Attenborough, David. *A Life on Our Planet: My Witness Statement and a Vision for the Future.* London: Witness Books, 2020.

81 Fink, Larry. "Larry Fink's 2021 letter to CEOs." BlackRock. January 26, 2021. Accessed September 9, 2021. https://www.blackrock.com/uk/individual/2021-larry-fink-ceo-letter

82 www.equator-principles.com

83 https://sdgs.un.org/goals

84 https://ec.europa.eu/info/business-economy-euro/banking-and-finance/sustainable-finance/eu-taxonomy-sustainable-activities_en Accessed May 17, 2022.

85 The National Archives. "Environmental Protection Act 1990." Legislation.gov.uk. Accessed September 13, 2021. https://www.legislation.gov.uk/ukpga/1990/43/contents

86 "Responsible Investing Around the World". Aberdeen Standard Investments, April 2020.

87 https://www.sasb.org/wp-content/uploads/2020/12/Press-release-prototype-climate-related-financial-disclosure-standard-Dec20-FINAL.pdf Accessed May 17, 2022.

88 Ibid.

89 Chouinard, Yvon and Stanley, Vincent. *The Responsible Company: What We've Learned from Patagonia's First 40 Years.* California: Patagonia Books, 2012.

90   Ibid.

91   "Reducing the use of natural resources in health and social care." 2018 report. Sustainable Development unit, NHS, Public Health England Centre for Sustainable healthcare

92 White, Andrew. "Lessons from Companies That Put Purpose Ahead of Short-Term Profits." Harvard Business Review. June 9, 2016. Accessed September 13, 2021. https://hbr.org/2016/06/lessons-from-companies-that-put-purpose-ahead-of-short-term-profits

## Chapter 12: Creating a control strategy

93   Ripley, Mark. "The Orange Book: Management of Risk – Principles and Concepts." Government Finance Function and HM Treasury. 2020. Accessed September 13, 2021. https://assets.publishing.service.gov.uk/government/uploads/system/uploads/attachment_data/file/866117/6.6266_HMT_Orange_Book_Update_v6_WEB.PDF

## Chapter 13: Governance and oversight

94   International Risk Governance Council. "What is Risk Governance?" International Risk Governance Council. Accessed September 13, 2021. https://irgc.org/risk-governance/what-is-risk-governance/

95   Quan, Ng Siew and Chiang, Alvin. "Taking The Right Risks: Risk Governance Defined." PricewaterhouseCoopers. Accessed September 13, 2021. https://www.pwc.com/sg/en/risk-assurance/assets/ra-sid-take-right-risks.pdf

96 Shield, Nicola, Elliott, Nick and Billinge, David. "Risk management in financial services." PricewaterhouseCoopers. 2012. Accessed September 13, 2021. https://pwc.blogs.com/files/risk-management-in-fs_pwc_north-1.pdf

97    Financial Conduct Authority. "Market Abuse Regulation." Financial Conduct Authority. May 5, 2016. Accessed September 13, 2021. https://www.fca.org.uk/markets/market-abuse/regulation

98 Financial Conduct Authority. "Senior Managers and Certification Regime." Financial Conduct Authority. July 6, 2015. Accessed September 13, 2021. https://www.fca.org.uk/firms/senior-managers-certification-regime

99 Financial Conduct Authority. "COCON 2.1 Individual conduct rules." Financial Conduct Authority. March 7, 2016. Accessed September 13, 2021. https://www.handbook.fca.org.uk/handbook/COCON/2/1.html?date=2016-06-30

100 Osborne, Andy. *Risk Management Simplified: A practical, step-by-step guide to identifying and addressing risks to your business.* Harvington, Worcestershire: HotHive Books, 2010.

## Chapter 14: Risk, data and information systems

101   Yaffe, Ellen, Strong, Jake and Zhu Beijing. "7 Key Actions for the Data-Driven Chief Risk Officer." Russell Reynolds Associates. October 26, 2020. Accessed September 13, 2021. https://www.russellreynolds.com/insights/thought-leadership/seven-key-actions-data-driven-cro

102   List partially sourced from Gartner, 2020.

103   Ibid.

104   Yaffe, Ellen, Strong, Jake and Zhu Beijing. "7 Key Actions for the Data-Driven Chief Risk Officer." Russell Reynolds Associates. October 26, 2020. Accessed September 13, 2021. https://www.russellreynolds.com/insights/thought-leadership/seven-key-actions-data-driven-cro

## Chapter 17: Putting it all together

105   Hancock, David. *Tame, Messy and Wicked Risk Leadership.* Abingdon, Oxon: Routledge, 2016.

106  FitchLearning, "The New Risk Paradigm: Non-Financial Risk Management." Fitchlearning.com. August 2020. Accessed January 26, 2022. https://your.fitch.group/rs/732-CKH-767/images/Fitch%20Learning_Research%20Report_NFRM.pdf

Printed in Great Britain
by Amazon

36228654R00132